INSTRUCTOR'S MANUAL TO ACCOMPANY

PASCAL
AND
TURBO PASCAL

Samuel L. Marateck

Courant Institute of Mathematical Sciences
New York University

John Wiley & Sons, Inc.

New York   Chichester   Brisbane   Toronto   Singapore

ISBN 0-471-53551-6

Printed in the United States of America

10 9 8 7 6 5 4 3 2 1

PREFACE

The teacher's manual contains many of the things we think a person teaching the Pascal course will need to teach it successfully. Since both texts, Pascal and Turbo Pascal, are accompanied by a set of disks containing the solutions to all the exercises in the books (Electronic Solutions Manual) and a set containing the programs (Programming Distribution Disks), the first section of this manual explains their use.

The next section contains all the answers to the short answer exercises. You may want to photocopy these pages and distribute the appropriate sections to your students as you assign each chapter to them.

The third section contains a description of how to use the tool boxes that are included with the distribution disks. A tool box is a set of general-use procedures that can be used to construct other programs.

For those of you who are using the texts as an adjunct to teaching non-programming courses, the fourth section contains a list of the interesting programs in the texts and their applications. The fifth section describes a series of programs in the texts constituting an example of programming abstraction. The sixth section consists of a syllabus for using Richard Pattis's "Karel the Robot" with the texts.

The seventh section describes some interesting projects that you can assign to your class. Finally, the eighth section discusses five case studies that because we didn't want the book to exceed a certain length, we excluded from the original plan for the texts. These case studies describe:

1. A global search and replace program that also reformats paragraphs.

2. A search for words following a given target word in a paragraph.

3. Long Integer arithmetic.

In order to expedite the publication of this manual, the case studies are included in their original galley format. This means that the figure numbers are thoses that would have been used if these studies were included in the texts. Also, the programs appear at the end of each case study.

It's a great pleasure to thank Rita Kerrigan for her expertise in producing this manual; and my colleagues Leah Beckman and Nathan Hull for adopting Pascal and Turbo Pascal respectively for their classes, solely on the basis of the galleys for the texts.

CONTENTS

How to use the Electronic Solutions Manual (ESM) and Program
Distribution Disk (PDD) for PASCAL & TURBO PASCAL by Samuel
L. Marateck.

WHAT ARE THE PDD AND ESM

The PDD contains all the programs in the books, and the ESM
contains all the answers to the questions.

WHAT THE PDD AND ESM CONTAIN

Both the ESM and PDD are divided into directories named CHAP3, CHAP4,
upto CHAP18, corresponding to Chapter 3 to 18 in the books. In the case
of Chapter 11, and only in this case, the directory CHAP11 includes the
files for PASCAL, whereas CHAP11T contains the files for TURBO PASCAL.
In general, if a program (FIG file) or exercise (EX file) has two
versions, one for PASCAL and one for TURBO PASCAL, their file names are
distinguishable by the letter "T". For instance, EX12.PAS, is the
version for PASCAL, and EXT12.PAS is the one for TURBO PASCAL.
Similarly, FIG12a.PAS, is the version for PASCAL, and FIGT12a.PAS is the
one for TURBO PASCAL. If there is only one version for both books, the
EX or FIG file applies to both. For example, for exercise 13, the file
is called EX13.PAS and there is no EXT13.PAS.

LOADING FILES FOR TURBO PASCAL FROM THE ESM AND PDD

1. Load the Turbo Pascal Compiler.

2. Place the ESM or Programming Disk in the 5-1/4" drive.

3. Hit the F10 key and select the File menu bar. Hit enter and then hit
   C to select "Change dir". A box will appear entitled "New Directory".
   Then if you want to select, for instance, CHAP11, (assuming the 5-1/4"
   drive is the A: drive), type

        a:\chap11

   (if the drive is the B: drive , type "b:\chap11".)

4. Hit the F3 key, and a box entitled "Load file name" will appear on
   the screen. Type
        .
   and a box entitled "B:\CHAP11*.*" will appear on the screen, with all
   the files in the directory. Select the desired program and run it.

   !!!It is very important that when you change the directory, you do it
   using the "Change dir" option and type in the "New directory" box, the
   name of the drive and the directory, e.g., "a:\chap15". If you change
   the directory from the "Load file" box by, for example, selecting a
   directory displayed in this box or by typing "a:\chap12*.*" and the
   selected program requires other files from the same directory, they will
   be unavailable because the path will not be correct. The Turbo Pascal
   compiler will still be in the original directory!!!

COPYING FILES FROM THE ESM AND PDD TO THE HARD DISK

1. In the root directory on the hard disk (you get there by typing, (CD\)
   form the directory CHAP3 by writing MKDIR CHAP3, then change to that
   directory by typing CD CHAP3

2. Insert the ESM in drive A: and change to that drive by typing A:
   Then change to directory CHAP3 on the ESM by writing CD CHAP3.

3. Copy all the files from Chapter 3 in the ESM to directory CHAP3
   on the hard disk by writing COPY *:* C:

4. If you want to copy all the files from the PDD onto directory CHAP3
   on the hard disk so that both the information for CHAP3 on the ESM
   and PDD will be there, do the following. Remove the ESM from drive
   A: and replace it with the PDD. Then type COPY *:* C: Otherwise,
   make a new directory on the hard disk, for instance, PDCHAP3, and
   copy all of files from CHAP3 on the PDD onto it.

5. Repeat steps 1. to 4. for the rest of the directories on the ESM
   and PDD.

LOADING FILES FOR TURBO PASCAL FROM THE ESM AND PDD DIRECTORIES
ON THE HARD DISK

1. Load the Turbo Pascal Compiler.

2. Hit the F10 key and select the File menu bar. Hit enter and then hit
   C to select "Change dir". A box will appear entitled "New Directory".
   Then if you want to select, for instance, CHAP11, type

        C:\chap11

   (If you made the CHAP directories, subdirectories of another directory
   that is in the root directory, say, TURBO6, you should type
   C:\TURBO6\chap11 instead)

3. Hit the F3 key, and a box entitled "Load file name" will appear on
   the screen. Type
        .
   and a box entitled "C:\CHAP11*.*" will appear on the screen, with all
   the files in the directory. Select the desired program and run it.

   !!!It is very important that when you change the directory, you do it
   using the "Change dir" option and type in the "New directory" box, the
   name of the directory, e.g., "C:\chap15". If you change
   the directory from the "Load file" box by, for example, selecting a
   directory displayed in this box or by typing "chap12*.*" and the
   selected program requires other files from the same directory, they will
   be unavailable because the path will not be correct. The Turbo Pascal
   compiler will still be in the original directory!!!

LOADING FILES FROM THE ESM AND PDD FOR STANDARD PASCAL SYSTEMS

If you are using a Pascal compiler in a Unix-like environment on a PC,
there are commands that will copy DOS ASCII files (the ones on the ESM
and PDD) to files that can be read by your compiler. If you are using a
main frame, you can use KERMIT or FTP to copy the ESM and PDD ASCII
files onto your system. Of course, the binary data files that are used
in Chapter 15 and are on the ESM and PDD will not be compatible with
non-DOS systems. You will have to use other programs on the ESM and PDD
to generate them.

The vast majority of the Standard Pascal programs on the ESM and PDD
will run on your Pascal compiler; however, a few, as we now describe,

will not run. The programs on the disks written for Standard Pascal and which use data files were written using the Turbo Pascal compiler so that they could be tested; Consequently, they contain statements that interface with DOS that are peculiar to Turbo Pascal, e.g., the ASSIGN and CLOSE statements. You will have to alter these statements to conform with your compiler. Also, all the programs dealing with Figure 8.5 were written using the RANDOM function and RANDOMIZE statement. You will also have to alter these statements to conform with your compiler.

Occaisonally, other Turbo Pascal statements will accidentally appear in a Standard Pascal program, for instance, USES and ClrScr. When you eliminate them, the program will run on your system.

4

The answers to the short answer exercises for Chapter 3

Exercise 1.

```
   -1
   -1
   -3
    0
   -1
```

Exercise 2.

Type	Value
real	5.0000000000E-01
real	2.5333333333E+01
integer	-10

Exercise 3.

1. "Type" is a reserved word.
2. In the Turbo Pascal version, the comment ends with a "]" instead of a "}"; however, the compiler indicates that perhaps an END is missing. Thus this error is difficult to detect.

   In the Pascal version, a "(*" should be used in place of "{" and a "*)", instead of "}" in the comment.
3. "VARIABLES" should be "VAR".
4. The "=" should be ":=".
5. "Velco" should be "Velocity".
6. "Velocity" and "Time" must be assigned values in order to calculate "Distance".

Exercise 4.

```
(a) A:= (3 + B) / (B + 2)
(b) R:= (3 * (A + B) * (A + B) - R) / 3
(c) C2:= A * A + B * B
```

Exercise 5.

The following should follow the first writeln,

```
readln(Length, Width, Price)
```

The program will compile because the missing readln is not a syntax error but it will cause the program to execute incorrectly.

Exercise 6.

It should be

```
writeln('John''s program')
```

Exercise 7.

```
writeln('''Hi there''')
```

Exercise 8.

    Only "tHINK" is a valid identifier.

Exercise 9.

    40 5.50

Exercise 10.

    A string, here 'Type the Time' cannot appear in a readln
    statement

Exercise 11.

  The output is:

  Total = 8.0000000000E+02

Note that the value 300 is first read into "Salary1", then the value 400
replaces it. Thus the sum is 400 + 400, or 800.

Exercise 12.

"File" and "Record" are reserved words and cannot be used as
identifiers.

Exercise 13.

    It is legal; however, the identifiers "readln" and "write"
    would no longer represent standard procedures.

The answers to the short answer exercises for Chapter 4.

Exercise 1.

  (a) You can not use a real expression for field width, it must be
      an integer expression. for instance 8 DIV 4.
  (b) The value 56 is an integer, thus you cannot specify a real
      field specification.
  (c) This is correct.

Exercise 2.

   37.500

Exercise 3.

          4.5654000000E+02
          4.6E+02
        456.54
        456.5400
              456.54

Exercise 4.

  (a) Standard Pascal: blank, carriage return, or non-numeric that is not
      part of the exponent.
      Turbo Pascal: blank or CR/LF
  (b) Standard Pascal: blank, carriage return, or non-numeric
      Turbo Pascal: blank or CR/LF
  (c) You may only read one character at a time into a character
      location. Thus there is no delimeter.
  (d) You can not read boolean values.

Exercise 5.

    readln(A, B, C, D, E, F, G, H)

Exercise 6.

  The value of "One" is 12.
  The value of "Two" is 13.
  The value of "Three" is 14
  The value of "Four" is 17.
  The value of "Five" is 18.
  The value of "Six" is 19.

Exercise 7.

  The value of "One" is 1.
  The value of "Two" is 2.
  The value of "Three" is a blank.
  The value of "Four" is 1.
  The value of "Five" is 7.
  The value of "Six" is a blank.

Exercise 8.

  The value of "One" is 1.
  The value of "Two" is is a blank.
  The value of "Three" is 2.

The value of "Four" is 3.
The value of "Five" is a blank because the carriage return was read.
The value of "Six" is 4.

In Turbo Pascal the results are the same except that the values of "Five" and "Six" are both blanks because the CR and LF are read.

Exercise 9.

The value of "Ch1" is 1.
The value of "Ch2" is is a blank.
The value of "Ch3" is 2.
The value of "Num1" is 34.
The value of "Num2" is 656.
The value of "Num3" is 8.

Exercise 10.

The value of "Num1" is 1.
The value of "Num2" is 234.
The value of "Num3" is 656
The value of "Ch1" is is a blank.
The value of "Ch2" is 8.
The value of "Ch3" is is a blank

Exercise 11.

Buffer   Variable read

```
|12 13 14 15 16~|
-----------------               Four
 ^
```

```
|12 13 14 15 16~|
-----------------               Five
   ^
```

```
|12 13 14 15 16~|
-----------------               Six
      ^
```

Exercise 12.

Buffer   Variable read

```
|12 13 14 15 16~|
-----------------               One
  ^
```

```
|12 13 14 15 16~|
-----------------               Two
    ^
```

```
|12 13 14 15 16~|
```

```
------------------                  Three
         ^


 |12  13  14  15  16˜|
 ------------------                  Four
              ^


 |12  13  14  15  16˜|
 ------------------                  Five
                   ^


 |17  18  19  20˜|
 --------------                      Six
 ^
```

The answers to the short answer exercises in Chapter 5:

Exercise 1.

Expression	Type	Value
succ('5')	Char	'6'
ord('3') - ord('0')	Integer	3
odd(pred(8))	Boolean	True
ord(chr(4))	Integer	4
chr(ord('3'))	Char	'3'
trunc(19.8)	Integer	19
round(19.8)	Integer	20
abs(3 + 6 MOD round(4.5) + 2)	Real	6.0

Exercise 2.

```
1  -150  -100
2   200   250
3  -150  -100
4   200   250
5  -150  -100
```

Exercise 3.

XXXXX-

Exercise 4.

```
1  3  2
1  2  3
2  3  1
2  1  3
3  2  1
3  1  2
```

Exercise 5.

Final value of Count = 12

The answers for the short answer exercises in Chapter 6:

Exercise 1.

```
Type your 5 factors
5 4 3 2 1
     120.00        1.00
```

Exercise 2.

```
Results of procedure
B= 6 C= 4 D= 4
Results of main program
A= 3 B= 4
```

Exercise 3.

```
Change values: X= 1 Y= 2 Z= 2
Main values: X= 1 Y= 0 Z= 2
```

Exercise 4.

In Standard Pascal only local variables can be used as loop control variables; and K is global.

Exercise 5.

Procedure Fact should precede Multiply since it is activated in Multiplier.

Exercise 6.

Factor is used both as a variable and as a procedure identifier.

Exercise 7.

In procedure Fact, the variable Product should be a VAR parameter.

Exercise 8.

Yes. The number of actual and formal parameters must be the same.

The answers to the short answer exercises in Chapter 7.

Exercise 1.

The expression 3 + A > B - 5 does not need parentheses because ">" is evaluated after the + and -. However, we must parenthesize (3 + R > B) AND Valid because the AND is evaluated first.

Exercise 2.

a. FALSE, b. FALSE, c. FALSE, d. FALSE

Exercise 3.

It is correct

Exercise 4.

8810241240
345678
2246610
5678910

Exercise 7.

a. Not valid because Mark 6 contains an embeded blank.
b. Valid
c. Not valid since 1 and 7 are not boolean expressions.
d. Not valid since the END is missing.
e. Valid
f. Valid

The answers to the short answer exercises for Chapter 8

Exercise 1.

For Standard Pascal, if the sample input is 3*2+4/2=, the output is 5. In Turbo Pascal, the sample input must have a blank following every operand, e.g., 3 *2 +4 /2 =, and every read(Operator) must be followed by a second read(Operator) to read the inserted blanks.

Exercise 2.

The program finds the square root of the input if the input is a perfect square. If its not, the program finds the square root of greatest perfect square that is less than the input. Thus an input of 10 produces a result 3.

Exercise 3.

The program reverse the order of the digits in the input.

Exercise 4.

The program determines how many digits an integer contains.

Exercise 5.

```
1   -200   -100
2    300    400
3   -200   -100
4    300    400
5   -200   -100
6    300    400
```

```
PROGRAM Ex5(input, output);
{Uses a WHILE loop}
VAR Index, Variable1, Variable2:integer;
BEGIN
    Variable1:= 300;
    Variable2:= 300;
    Index:=1;
    WHILE Index < 7 DO BEGIN
        Variable1:= 100 - Variable1;
        Variable2:= 100 + Variable1;
        writeln(Index:4, Variable1:6, Variable2:6);
        Index:= Index + 1
    END (* Index *)
END.


PROGRAM Ex5(input, output);
{Uses a REPEAT loop}
VAR Index, Variable1, Variable2:integer;
BEGIN
    Variable1:= 300;
    Variable2:= 300;
    Index:=1;
    REPEAT
```

```
                Variable1:= 100 - Variable1;
                Variable2:= 100 + Variable1;
                writeln(Index:4, Variable1:6, Variable2:6);
                Index:= Index + 1
            UNTIL Index > 6
        END.
```

Exercise 6.

```
    Type your integers on one line
    5 10 15 10 5 5 0 10 7 5
    Sum = 25 InputValue = 0
```

Exercise 7.

    a. Invalid: missing a DO.
    b. Valid; but standard function eoln is redefined.
    c. Valid.
    d. Valid.
    e. Valid.
    f. Invalid: missing an UNTIL; the BEGIN and END are
       unnecessary.

Exercise 8.

   Before the execution starts, there is nothing in the buffer so
   the program waits for input.

Exercise 9.

   Since a read precedes the loop and the reading of a period
   terminates the loop, the counter counts the character read in the
   previous execution of the loop.

   Since the execution of one of these statements does not effect the
   execution of the the other one, we may interchange these two
   statements in the loop.

Exercise 10.

   If execution of a statement changes the values of the variables
   in another statement, then interchanging the order of the statements
   will produce a different final result. For example, changing the
   order of the statements

```
        A:= A + 1;
        B:= 2 * A
```

will generate different results.

Exercise 11.

    (a) Change the eoln(Data) to eof(Data), otherwise you will read only
        one number.
    (b) No changes needed.
    (c) If Number is declared integer, in Turbo no changes are needed.
        Since the characters are written on the file contiguously, one
        execution of the readln will read the entire file. On the other
        hand, if Number is declared real, the computer in Standard and
        Turbo Pasacl will only read the first number even if you replace
```
```

the eoln(Data) with eof(Data).

Exercise 19.

Because of roundoff error, the result is not precise.

The answers to the short answer exercises in Chapter 9.

Exercise 1.

1. The function does not have a type.
2. The function name does not appear in the righthand side of an assignment statement.

Exercise 2.

The function name appears with out a parameter in the writeln statement.

Exercise 3.

Yes, it is correct.

Exercise 4.

The function name appears on the right hand side of the ':=" without a parameter.

Exercise 5.

It does not evaluate Digit1 raised to the zeroth power correctly.

The answers to the short answer exercises in Chapter 10

Exercise 1.

```
 -2
  0
 -6
 -8
-10
```

Exercise 2.

```
J= 1 Ray = 2
J= 2 Ray = 8
J= 3 Ray = 18
J= 4 Ray = 32
J= 5 Ray = 50
J= 6 Ray = 72
J= 7 Ray = 98
J= 8 Ray = 128
J= 9 Ray = 162
J= 10 Ray = 200
```

Exercise 3.

(a) Should be VAR Ray:ARRAY[1..5] OF integer;
(b) Valid
(c) Valid
(d) A subscript cannot be a real. Two dots not three should separate the dimension limits.
(e) Valid
(f) Valid

Exercise 4.

Since 'X' follows 'O' in the collating sequence, the array is incorrectly dimensioned. It should be ARRAY[O..X]

The answers to the short answer exercises to Chapter 11

Exercise 1.

   4

Exercise 2.

  aabbb

Exercise 3.

  aaabbbb

Exercise 4.

  Copy(StringA, 4, 3) assuming that StringA is the result of exercise 3.

Exercise 5. (For Turbo Pascal only)

  The INTERFACE section is the public part of the unit. It contains the declarations and definitions that can be used by the host and the subprograms in the unit itself. The IMPLEMENATION section, on the other hand, contains only the definitions and declarations that can be used in the UNIT.

Exercise 6. (For Turbo Pascal only)

  You might want the subprograms in the unit to use the declarations and subprograms in another unit.

  If USES occurs in the INTERFACE section, then not only can the activating unit use the information in the other activated unit, but the original host can use them as well. On the other hand, if the USES occurs in the IMPLEMENTATION section, then only the subprograms in the activating unit can use the information.

The answers to the short answer exercises for Chapter 12

Exercise 1.

   You are not allow to repeat a constant (here, T) in the definition.

Exercise 2.

   An identifier cannot (here, Dodge City and Garden City) contain an
   embedded blank.

Exercise 3.

   You cannot use a text constant (for example, 'Saturday') in the
   definition of an enumerated type.

Exercise 4.

```
Line 1 4 5 3 4 2 3 1 2
Line 2 : 1 2
Line D  1 8 1 4
Line D -3 9 0 7
Line 3 : 9 5 3 7
```

The answers to the short answer exercises in Chapter13

Exercise 1.

Assuming the procedure heading is "PROCEDURE FormWord(Letter:List);", the contents of Letter is Den.

Exercise 2.

```
PROGRAM Ex2;
TYPE List = ARRAY[1..10] OF char;
     City = ARRAY[1..4] OF List;
VAR CityName: City;
    J: integer;

BEGIN
    CityName[2]:= 'ABCDEFGHIK';
    FOR J:= 1 TO 7 DO
        write( CityName[2, J] )
END.
```

Exercise 3.

The type of CityName is of course City, but more important, the type of Temp should be List.

Exercise 4.

The selector, State, must be of ordinal type. Here it's type is an array of character.

The answers to the short answer exercises in Chapter 14.

Exercise 1.

The definition of NameType shoulc preceed the record definition

Exercise 2.

In Turbo Pascal, the field Name should be defined as string[20]. In Standard Pascal, the field Name should be defined as PACKED ARRAY[1..20] OF char;

Exercise 3.

EmployeeName.Name.MiddleInitial:='L', where we are assuming that "L" is the middle initial.

Exercise 4.

```
WITH EmployeeName DO
   Name.MiddleInitial:='L',
```

 or

```
WITH EmployeeName DO
   WITH Name DO
        MiddleInitial:='L',
```

where "L" is the middle initial.

Exercise 5.

WITH EmployeeName, NameRecord DO is incorrect since NameRecord is a Type and not a field

WITH Name, EmployeeName DO is incorrect because Name is a field of EmployeeName record.

Exercise 6.

No. Even though the fields and definitions of StudentRec and ExamRec are identical, they have different Type names.

Exercise 7.

The Type of Life is not defined. It must be defined in the CASE part of the variant record.

Exercise 8.

NumOfRecords:= NumOfRecords + 1 must appear between the WHILE and the WITH. As it appears now, it changes the meaning of Present[NumOfRecords] in the readln.

The answers to the short answer exercises in Chapter 15.

Exercise 1.

LibraryFile is a TYPE and not a variable identifier.

Exercise 2.

You cannot use a writeln with a structured file.

Exercise 3.

It should be: write(LibraryFile, Info). You may only use a record identifier to follow the file identifier as the parameters of the write and read statements for a file.

Exercise 4.

Since the subscript of the middle element is obtained from Middle:= (First + Last) DIV 2, the first value of Middle here is 3. So the record the matches "Abrams" is "Abrahams Samuel 7".

Exercise 5.

"<" is not a valid set operation.

Exercise 6.

(a) [1, 2, 3, 6, 7, 9], (b) [1, 2, 7], (c) [3]

Exercise 7.

(a) True, (b) False (c) Type mismatch

Exercise 8.

SetA is originally undefined

Exercise 9.

Letter IN ['A'..'Z', 'a'..'z']

Exercise 10.

False since there are characters between "Z" and "a" in the ASCII Table.

The answers to the short answer questions in Chapter 16.

Exercise 1.

A local variable will be stored on the stack for each successive call, whereas a global variable will not.

Exercise 2.

```
6      9
-2     2
5     11
```

The answers to the short answer exercises in Chapter 17.

Exercise 1.

You may not dereference the pointer, i.e., you cannot refer to the contents of the location that Q points to; for example, Q^.Next is not allowable when the value of Q is NIL.

Exercise 2.

Q^ contains an arbitrary value since nothing has been stored there

Exercise 3.

Since Q points to the same address as P, Q^ contains the value 4.

Exercise 4.

When you pass a pointer as a value parameter, any changed made to the pointer's value in the activated procedure is not transferred to the activating procedure. Any change made to the contents of the location the pointer points to, however, is transferred. For instance if Q is an actual value parameter, and P is the corresponding formal parameter, if P^.Next is set to NIL in the activated procedure, the value of Q^.Next will also be NIL.

When you pass a pointer as a variable parameter, however, not only are changed made to the location the pointer points to, transferred to the activating program; but also changes made to the pointer's value are transferred.

Exercise 5.

When the value of Stack is NIL, the statement

    Stack:= Stack^.NextAddress

will cause an error since NIL^.NextAddress (dereferencing NIL), will cause an error.

Exercise 6.

The value of Character is undefined; however since the WHILE loop in the main program is not executed when Stack = NIL, procedure POP will not be activated.

The answers to the short answer exercises in Chapter 18.

Exercise 1.

Since the list is created in Build, the address of the (first) node will nor be transferred to the main program unless List is a VAR parameter.

Exercise 2.

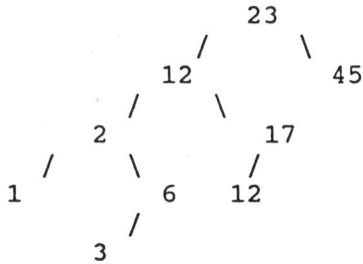

```
                23
              /    \
           12        45
          /  \
        2      17
       / \     /
      1   6   12
           \
            3
```

Exercise 3.

a. (45+)*(39-) -> 45+39-*

b.   2*3-(4+(53-)*6-32$)
     23*-(4+(53-6*)-32$)
     23*-(453-6*+32$-
     23*453-6*+32$--→

Exercise 4.

Inorder traversal: FCBASD
Postorder traversal: FBCSDA
Preorder traversal: ACFBDS

Exercise 5.

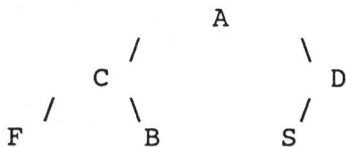

```
              A
            /    \
       C             D
      /  \          /
    F      B      S
```

Exercise 6.

(a)

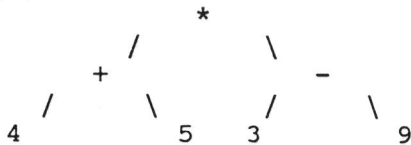

```
              *
            /    \
         +          -
        /  \      /   \
      4      5   3      9
```

(b)

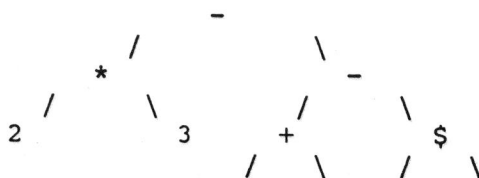

```
              -
            /    \
         *          -
        /  \      /   \
      2      3   +      $
                / \    / \
```

```
      4        *  3        2
              /   \
           -       6
          /     \
        5         3
```

Exercise 7.

    Nothing is wrong with it. Sorry.

TOOL BOXES

Tool boxes are groups of procedures, some of which are taken from the book, that enable the student to write complicated programs requiring these procedures without having to write these procedures from scratch.

`*********************************************`

TOOL BOX UTILITY (Found in ESM directory CHAP10)

Tool box UTILITY is used in Chapter 10 to read and sort integers. It contains the following procedures:

PROCEDURE ReadElem(VAR List:IntArray; VAR Count:SubRange);
{reads integers typed on a line into an array. Count is the number of items read}

PROCEDURE Sort(VAR List: IntArray; NumElem: Subrange);
{Sorts a list consisting of NumElem elements}

PROCEDURE Print(List:IntArray; Count:Subrange);
{Prints a list consisting of Count items}

An example of the TYPE and CONST definitions used with UTILITY are:

```
CONST MaxSubsc=100;
TYPE IntArray = ARRAY[1..MaxSubsc] OF integer;
     SubRange = 0..MaxSubsc;
```

Given VAR List:IntArray; Count:SubRange; an example of the sequence of statements that would read, sort, and then print a sequence of integer values are:

```
    ReadElem(List, Count);
    Sort(List, Count);
    Print( List, Count)
```

For example, the following input

34 1 2 7 32 8

would produce the following output:

1 2 7 8 32 34

`*********************************************`

TOOL BOX CARUTIL1 (Found in PDD directory CHAP15)

Tool box CARUTIL1 is used in Chapter 15 to:

1. produce 52 unique random integers corresponding to the cards in a shuffled deck of cards
2. print the 52 random integers.

It contains the following procedures:

PROCEDURE Print(Deck: Full_Deck);
{Prints Deck}

PROCEDURE Zero(VAR Dealt: Was_Dealt);
{Zeros Dealt aray}

```
PROCEDURE Shuffle(Dealt: Was_Dealt; VAR Deck: Full_Deck);
{Shuffles deck}
```

An example of the TYPE and CONST definitions used with CARUTIL1 are:

```
TYPE Range = 1..52;
     Was_Dealt = ARRAY[Range] OF boolean;
     Full_Deck = ARRAY[Range] OF Range;
```

Given VAR Dealt:Was_Dealt; Deck:Full_Deck; an example of the sequence of
statements that would produce 52 unique random integers corresponding to
the cards in a shuffled deck of cards are:

```
    Zero(Dealt);
    Shuffle(Dealt, Deck);
    Print(Deck)
```

```
*******************************************
```
TOOL BOXES ZEROHAND, DEALHAND AND PRINTNAM (Found in PDD directory CHAP15)

These tool boxes are also used in Chapter 15. They display the cards
dealt in NumOfHand hand of cards.

TOOL BOX ZEROHAND

Its places zeros in the 4 X 13 matrices describing the NumOfHands hands
of cards. Its heading is:

```
PROCEDURE Zero_Hands(VAR Results:Hands);
```

TOOL BOX DEALHAND

It deals NumOfHands hands consisting of NumPerHand cards
from the shuffled deck. Its heading is:

```
PROCEDURE Deal_Hands(VAR Results:Hands; Deck: Full_Deck);
```

TOOL BOX PRINTNAM

This procedure prints the names of the ordinal values corresponding
to the Suit and Face values. Its heading is:

```
PROCEDURE PrintName(Suit:SuitType; Face:FaceType);
```

```
*******************************************
```
TOOL BOX CARUTIL2 (Found in PDD directory CHAP15)

This is also used in Chapter 15. Procedures WinFace and WinSuit
detect lays in the game rummy in two seven-card hands. Their
headings are:

```
PROCEDURE WinFace(Results:Hands; I:Hand);
{Determines whether there is a lay of 3 or more consecutive cards}
```

```
PROCEDURE WinSuit(Results:Hands; I:Hand);
{Determines whether there is a lay for a given face}
```

```
PROCEDURE Print_Cards(Results:Hands);
{Prints the face and suit value of the cards dealt for NumOfHands hands
```

and then calls WinFace and WinSuit}

An example of the TYPE and CONST definitions used with ZEROHAND,
DEALHAND AND PRINTNAM CARUTIL2 are:

```
CONST NumPerHand = 7;
      NumOfHands = 2;
TYPE Range = 1..52;
     WasDealt = ARRAY[Range] OF boolean;
     FullDeck = ARRAY[Range] OF Range;
     FaceType = (Two, Three, Four, Five, Six, Seven, Eight, Nine,
                 Ten, Jack, Queen, King, Ace);
     SuitType = (Clubs, Spades, Hearts, Diamonds);
     Binary = 0..1;
     Hands = ARRAY[1..NumOfHands, Clubs.. Diamonds, Two..Ace] OF integer;
     Hand = 1..NumOfHands;
```

Given VAR Dealt: WasDealt; Deck: FullDeck; Results:Hands; an example of the
sequence of statements that would shuffle a deck of cards, deal NumOfHand hands
of NumPerHand cards, check for lays in the game rummy and print the results are:

```
     Zero(Dealt);
     Shuffle(Dealt, Deck);
     Print(Deck);
     Zero_Hands(Results);
     Deal_Hands(Results, Deck);
     Print_Cards(Results)
```

An example of the sequence of statements that would only shuffle a deck of
cards, and deal NumOfHand of NumPerHand cards, i.e., setup the NumOfHand
4 X 13 matrices containing 1's in the appropriate positions for the cards
dealt and zeros elsewhere is:

```
     Zero(Dealt);
     Shuffle(Dealt, Deck);
     Print(Deck);
     Zero_Hands(Results);
     Deal_Hands(Results, Deck);
```

```
*******************************************
```
TOOL BOX STRUTIL (Found in both PDD & ESM directory CHAP11)

This tool box contains the string procedures described in Chapter 11 of the
PASCAL version of the book. The procedure headings are:

FUNCTION Length(InString:Line):integer;

PROCEDURE Print(InString:Line);

PROCEDURE Copy(InString:Line; VAR Substring:Line;
               Index, Count:integer);
(* Copies a substring to a string *)
(* "Index" is starting point & "Count" is length *)

PROCEDURE ReadString(VAR FileA:text; VAR InString:Line);
(* Reads characters into string array *)

FUNCTION Pos(Substring, InString:Line):integer;
(* Finds position in string of substring; returns 0 if not found *)

```
PROCEDURE Delete(VAR InString:Line; Index, Count:integer);
(* Deletes characters from string *)

PROCEDURE Insert(SubString:Line; VAR InString:Line;
                 Index:integer);
(* Inserts characters in string *)
```

Subprograms Pos, Delete, Insert and Length also have the same form as the Turbo Pascal functions with the same name.

****
TOOL BOX BUILD (Found in ESM directory CHAP17)

This tool box generates and prints a linked list containing 9 nodes. The headings are:

```
PROCEDURE Print(P: Pointer);
{Prints a linked list}

PROCEDURE Build(VAR List:Pointer);
{Produces a linked list}
```

An example of the TYPE definitions used with BUILD are:

```
TYPE Pointer = ^Node;
     Node = RECORD
              Data: integer;
              next: Pointer
     END;
```

Given VAR List:Pointer; an example of the sequence of statements that would generate and then print the linked list are:

```
         Build(List);
         Print(List)
```

The numbers in the nodes are the digits from 1 to 9.
****
TOOL BOX BUILD2 (Found in ESM directory CHAP17)

This is the same as tool box BUILD except that now the list is a doulbly linked list. The headings are:

```
PROCEDURE Print(P: Ptr);
{Prints a linked list}

PROCEDURE Build(VAR List:Ptr);
{Produces a linked list}
```

An example of the TYPE definitions used with BUILD2 are:

```
TYPE Ptr = ^Node;
     Node = RECORD
          Data:integer;
          Left, Right:Ptr
     END {Node};
```

Given VAR List:Ptr; an example of the sequence of statements that would generate and then print the linked list are:

```
        Build(List);
        Print(List)
```

```
*******************************************
```
TOOL BOX BUILD3 (Found in ESM directory CHAP17)

This tool box contains the subprograms used to generate and
print a linked list using static pointers. See Static Pointers on Page
790 and exercises 14 to 22 on page 791 of the TURBO PASCAL text; Also
see Static Pointers on Page 763 and exercises 14 to 22 on page 764 of
the TURBO PASCAL text. The headings of the procedures are:

```
FUNCTION GetNode: Link;
{Removes a node from the available list}
{Similar to NEW with dynamic pointers}
```

```
PROCEDURE Print(P:Link);
```

```
PROCEDURE Create(VAR Avail: Link; VAR Node:ArrayNode);
{Create the Available List}
```

```
PROCEDURE BuildList(VAR List, Avail:Link; VAR Node:ArrayNode);
{Generates a linked list}
```

```
*******************************************
```
TOOL BOX TREE   (Found in ESM directory CHAP18)

This is the tool box for making a binary tree with integer nodes.
Uses recursion to create the tree. Also contains Height function
and Inorder traversal procedure. The procedure headings are:

```
FUNCTION SubTree(X: integer): Nodeptr;
{Creates a tree with a node and two NIL children}
```

```
PROCEDURE LeftTree(P:Nodeptr; X:integer);
{Inserts a node as the left child for pointer P}
```

```
PROCEDURE RightTree(P:Nodeptr; X:integer);
{Inserts a node as the right child for pointer P}
```

```
PROCEDURE Intrav( Tree:Nodeptr);
{Prints the nodes of a tree in infix order}
```

```
FUNCTION Height(T:NodePtr):integer;
{Finds height of a tree}
```

```
PROCEDURE InsertTree(VAR Tree:NodePtr; Data:integer);
(* Creates a binary search tree *)
```

```
PROCEDURE BinaryTree(VAR Tree:NodePtr);
(* Reads data and activates tree creation procedure *)
```

An example of the TYPE definitions used with TREE are:

```
TYPE NodePtr = ^Parent;
     Parent = RECORD
                info: integer;
                Left, Right: NodePointer
     END;
```

Given VAR Tree: NodePtr; an example of the sequence of statements that would generate, print the contents of the nodes and then find the height of a binary search tree, are:

```
BinaryTree(Tree);
writeln('An inorder traversal of the tree yields');
InTraversal(tree);
writeln('The height of the tree is ', Height(Tree) )
```

The data can be written in any order, on one line, e.g.,

12 4 3 2 17 56 2

****
TOOL BINTREE (Found in ESM directory CHAP18)

This produces a binary search using iteration. It uses SubTree, LeftTree, and RightTree from tool box TREE. The procedure heading is:

PROCEDURE BinTree(VAR TreePointer:NodePtr);
{Produces a binary search using iteration}

An example of the TYPE definitions used with BINTREE are:

```
TYPE NodePtr = ^Parent;
     Parent = RECORD
               info: integer;
               Left, Right: NodePointer
     END;
```

Given VAR Tree: NodePtr; an example of the sequence of statements that would generate, print the contents of the nodes and then find the height of the binary search tree, are:

```
BinTree(Tree);
writeln('An inorder traversal of the tree yields');
InTraversal(tree);
writeln('The height of the tree is ', Height(Tree) )
```

The data can be written in any order, on one line, e.g.,

12 4 3 2 17 56 2

****
TOOL BOX CHARTREE (Found in ESM directory CHAP18)

This is the tool box for making a binary tree with character nodes. It is identical to tool box TREE except that the "Info" field is of CHAR type, i.e.,

```
TYPE NodePtr = ^Parent;
     Parent = RECORD
               info: integer;
               Left, Right: NodePointer
     END;
```

The procedure headings are:

FUNCTION SubTree(X: char): Nodeptr;

```
PROCEDURE LeftTree(P:Nodeptr; X:char);

PROCEDURE RightTree(P:Nodeptr; X:char);

PROCEDURE Intrav( Tree:Nodeptr);

FUNCTION Height(T:NodePtr):integer;

PROCEDURE InsertTree(VAR Tree:NodePtr; Data:char);
(* Creates a binary search tree *)

PROCEDURE BinaryTree(VAR Tree:NodePtr);
(* Reads data and activates tree creation procedure *)
```

Given VAR Tree: NodePtr; an example of the sequence of statements that would generate, print the contents of the nodes and then find the height of the binary search tree for lower case letters, are:

```
        BinTree(Tree);
        writeln('An inorder traversal of the tree yields');
        InTraversal(tree);
        writeln('The height of the tree is ', Height(Tree) )
```

The data can be written in any order, on one line, e.g.,

acdgfed

```
**********************************************
```
TOOL BOX EXPRESS (Found in ESM directory CHAP18)

This is the tool box for making an expression tree. Also contains the Height function and Inorder traversal procedure. The headings are:

```
FUNCTION Pop( VAR S: StackPointer):NodePointer;
(* Pops pointer to a node from linked-list stack *)

PROCEDURE Push( VAR S:StackPointer; Pointer:NodePointer);
(* Pushes pointer to a node on linked-list stack *)

FUNCTION Operand (Token: char): boolean;
(* Determines whether or not a token is an operand *)

FUNCTION Operator (Token: char): boolean;
(* Determines whether or not a token is an operator *)

FUNCTION SubTree(x:char): NodePointer;

PROCEDURE InTraversal( tree:NodePointer);

PROCEDURE BinaryExpressTree(VAR Tree:NodePointer);
(* creates a binary expression tree *)

FUNCTION Height(T:NodePointer):integer;
```

An example of the TYPE and CONST definitions used with EXPRESS are:

```
CONST Blank = ' ';
      LeftParens = ')';

TYPE          NodePointer =^Parent;
```

```
            Parent = RECORD
                    Info:char;
                    Right, Left: NodePointer
            END;
            StackPointer = ^Stack;
            Stack = RECORD
               Info: NodePointer;
              Next:StackPointer
            END;
            Error = (OK, MissingLeftParens, TooManyLeftParens, BadToken);
```

Given

```
VAR  Tree: NodePointer;
     S: StackPointer;
     Code: Error;
```

an example of the sequence of statements that would generate an expression tree, are:

```
    S:= NIL; (* Stack *)
    writeln('Type your over-parenthesised expression and then a C.R.');
    BinaryExpressTree(Tree, S, Code);
    ActOnCode(Code)
```

where procedure ActOnCode is given by:

```
PROCEDURE ActOnCode(Code:Error);
(* Performs proper action depending on value of Code *)
BEGIN
  CASE Code OF
      OK:                 BEGIN
                              write('Infix traversal of tree ');
                              InTraversal(Tree)
                          END (* OK *);
      MissingLeftParens: writeln('Faulty input. Missing at least one "("  ');
      TooManyLeftParens: writeln('Faulty input. Too many  "(" s  ');
      BadToken: writeln('Bad token encountered')
   END (* CASE *)
END (* ActOn Code *);
```

The data must be a fully parenthesized infix expression, e.g.,

((2+5)/(3^8))

****
TOOL BOX STRITREE (Found in ESM directory CHAP18)

This tool box makes a binary search tree with string nodes. Uses recursion
 to create the tree. Also contains Height function and Inorder
 traversal procedure. The headings are:

```
FUNCTION SubTree(X: string): Nodeptr;

PROCEDURE LeftTree(P:Nodeptr; X:string);

PROCEDURE RightTree(P:Nodeptr; X:string);

PROCEDURE Intrav( Tree:Nodeptr);
```

```
FUNCTION Height(T:NodePtr):integer;

PROCEDURE InsertTree(VAR Tree:NodePtr; Data:string);
(* Creates a binary search tree *)

PROCEDURE BinaryTree(VAR Tree:NodePtr);
(* Reads data and activates tree creation procedure *)
```

An example of the TYPE definitions used with STRITREE are:

```
TYPE Nodeptr = ^Nodetype;
     Nodetype = record
                  info: string;
                  Left, Right: Nodeptr
     END;
```

Given VAR TreePointer: NodePtr; an example of the sequence of statements that would generate, print the contents of the nodes and then find the height of the binary search tree for lower case strings, are:

```
    BinTree(TreePointer);
    writeln('An inorder traversal of the tree yields');
    intrav(TreePointer);
    writeln('The height of the tree is ', Height(TreePointer) )
```

The data can be written in any order, one lowercase string per line, e.g.,

```
drink
eat
devour
fast
feast
^Z
```

where the ^Z indicates an end of file.

```
********************************************
```
TOOL BOX QUEUES (Found in ESM directory CHAP18)

This is the tool box for creating a queue in which the nodes are the nodes of trees: The headings are:

```
FUNCTION Empty(Q: Queue):boolean;
(* Tests for ampty queue *)

PROCEDURE Append(VAR Q: Queue; TreePtr: NodePtr);
(* Inserts node at beginning of the queue *)

PROCEDURE Remove(VAR Q: Queue; VAR TreePtr: NodePtr);
(* Removes the front item from the queue *)
```
The solution to Exercise 28 in Chapter 18 shows how this is used:

```
PROGRAM EX28;
(* Performs a breadth first search *)
CONST Blank = ' ';

TYPE (* Records for trees *)
    NodePtr = ^Parent;
    Parent = RECORD
```

```
                        Depth: integer;
                        Info: integer;
                        Left, Right: NodePtr
                     END;
          (* Records for queues *)
          Pointer = ^Node;
          Node = RECORD
                    DataPart: NodePtr;
                    NextAddress: Pointer
                 END (* Node *);
          Queue = RECORD
                    Front, Rear:Pointer
                  END (* Queue *);

VAR Tree: NodePtr;


{$I Queues}

{$I Tree }
{Activates: BinaryTree, Intrav, SubTree, LeftTree, and RightTree}

PROCEDURE BreadthSearch(Root:NodePtr);
{Performs a breadth first search}
VAR Q:Queue;
    Tree:NodePtr;
BEGIN
     WITH Q DO
           Front:= NIL;
     writeln('A breadth first search yields:');
     Tree:= Root; {Allows you to work with Tree later; else Tree is NIL}
     Append(Q, Tree);
     WHILE NOT Empty(Q) DO BEGIN
           Remove(Q, Tree);
           IF Tree <> NIL THEN BEGIN
              (* Note leaves have NIL as children *)
              write(Tree^.Info:3);
              Append(Q, Tree^.Left);
              Append(Q, Tree^.Right)
           END (* IF *)
     END (* WHILE *)
END (* BreadthFirst *);

BEGIN
     BinaryTree(Tree);
     BreadthSearch(Tree)
END.
```

Programs of special interest in PASCAL & TURBO PASCAL

Description	Application	PASCAL	TURBO PASCAL
Adding two numbers with "$"s and ","s	Real life simu-lation.	258-265	288-295
Random walk	Program design & planning	314-323 Also last program on Demo disk	344-353
Standard deviation	Statistics	408-420	436-447
Frequency of letters used in a sentence	Linguistics	420-435	448-463
Printing the frequencies of letters so they are sorted by frequency	Linguistics	598-607	620-629
Search & replace	Word processor Generalized program appears as first program on Demo disk.	Chap 11	Ch 11
Printing Roman numerals	Enumerated type	500-506	524-529
Generating a calendar	Enumerated type	494-499	518-523
Finding distance between two cities	Table look-up program	520-537	544-559
Sorting words read from a paragraph	Sorting	544-551	566-573
Sorting records on a key	Data base	594-599	616-620
Forming an index	Stable sorts	606-617	628-639
Simulating the card game Rummy	Simulation Appears as third program on demo disk.	644-662	666-682
Binary search	Searching	663-667	682-690
Buckets & well problem	Classic problem in recursion	701-744	725-730
Generating an expression tree	Compiler design		812-818

PROGRAMMING ABSTRACTION

One of the important results of programming abstraction applies to
sorting records: Once the sort procedure is correctly written it can be
used to sort records composed of any types, i.e. it can sort on a name
(string type), ID (integer type) or an enumerated type. You determine
the key on which the sort is done by writing the RECORD definition in
the main program or appropriate UNIT. Thus if the heading is

```
PROCEDURE Sort(VAR Account:Grid; NumElements:Range)
```

and the type is:

```
TYPE RecordType = RECORD
        Branch, Key:integer;
        Deposit:real
      END {RecordType};
Grid = ARRAY[1..100] OF RecordType
```

the sorting will be done on an integer key. Whereas, if the definition
is rewritten as:

```
TYPE RecordType = RECORD
        Branch:integer;
        Key:String[20];
        Deposit:real
      END {RecordType};
Grid = ARRAY[1..100] OF RecordType
```

the sorting will be done an a string key without your needing to alter
the sorting procedure.

See Sections
13.3, 13.4, 14.6 and 14.9.

Syllabus for using Pascal with Karel The Robot

Chapters from Karel The Robot, by Richard Pattis, Wiley, 1981

Chapter 1 to 4
Chapter 5, Section 5.1 to 5.5

Sections from Pascal by S. Marateck, Wiley 1991

Chapter 2, Program Planning (Review of what's discussed in Karel
the Robot viz this subject.)

Chapter 3, An Introduction to Pascal, Sec 3.1 to 3.16
Chapter 4, Reading & Writing, Sec 4.1 to 4.2, 4.5, 4.7(Optional)
Chapter 5, Sec 5.1 to 5.7, 5.8(Optional), 5.9(Optional), 5.10, 5.11
Chapter 6, Sec 6.1 to 6.5
Chapter 7, Sec 7.1 to 7.11, 7.13(Optional)
Chapter 8, Sec 8.1 to 8.3, 8.5
Chapter 9, Sec 9.1 to 9.3
Chapter 10, Sec 10.1, 10.2, 10.5

ADDITONAL PROJECTS

1. In Chapter 11 the PASCAL text describes different string processing functions (i.e.., position, insert, delete, copy and length) and the exercises at the end of Chapter 11 in the Turbo Pascal text asks you to write these functions Complete this list of functions by writing a procedure that compares two strings for alphabetical order and one that concatenates them. This would now represent an example of abstracted data type because it consists of a type (here, a string) and operations on the type (i.e, position, insert, delete, copy, compare srings for alphabetical order, length, and concatenation).

2. Using dynamic pointers, write a program that performs all the string processing functions described in Project 1 on a linked list which has nodes whose data parts contain a character.

3. Write a program that converts a Roman numeral into its decimal equivalent.

4. Write a program that mimics the lisiting of the DOS directory. The directory should be a linked list in which the data part of the node contains the name and extension of the file and the file's length in bytes. The operations on the list should be:

   ADD. This adds the file's name (e.g., Prog1.pas) and length (e.g., 256) to the linked list representing the directory. The operation is performed by ADD(Prog1.pas, 256)

   ERASE. This removes a node from the directory. For instance, ERASE(Prog1.pas) removes the node representing Progr1.pas from the directory. Impliment this so that you can use wild card characters. Thus ERASE(*.pas) would remove all nodes with extensions "pas" and ERASE(*.*) would erase all the nodes. Of course when this form of the ERASE is used, the program should ask, "Do you want to erase all the nodes? Y or N".

   DIR. This lists the directory. DIR(*.*) lists all the entries. DIR(*.pas) would list all the entries with extension "pas". The end of the listing should indicate the amount of bytes used and the amount left.

   The maximum number of entries in the directory should not exceed 64, and the maximum number of acumulated bytes should be 360K.

5. Alter Project 5 so that is also creates (MKDIR) removes (RMDIR) and changes (CD) the directory. Then DIR(*.*) would list the names of the files in the current directory, CD.. would change to the parent directory, etc. Just as in DOS, your program should not allow the removal of a directory that contains any program nodes.

15.2

REFORMATTING A PARAGRAPH READ FROM A FILE

BEFORE YOU BEGIN

Have you ever wondered how a word processing program formats a paragraph such that each line starts in, for instance, column 10 and no word in the line extends beyond, let's say, column 70? We now show how this is done.

The next program takes a paragraph written on a text file and reformats it so that the paragraph is written between two specified columns read by the program. For example, if the beginning of the paragraph is

```
My country tis of thee,
Sweet land of liberty,
Of thee I sing.
```

and we specify that the paragraph should appear between columns 12 and 42, then the beginning of the reformatted paragraph appears as follows:

```
12345678901234567890123456789012345678901234567890123456789012345678901234567890
    My country tis of thee, Sweet
    land of liberty, Of thee I
    sing.
```

This includes a calibration of the column numbers so that you can check that the paragraph has been typed between the proper columns. Do you remember the data structures we used in the program that read a text file into a two-dimensional array (Figure 13.7a)

```
TYPE Line = array[1..80] of char;
     Page = array[1..20] of Line;
```

where Line describes the array into which each line on the file is read and Page describes the array of lines? Since these data structures are appropriate for the present problem, we'll use them here. We'll also use

```
EndOfLine = array[1..20] of integer;
```

where **EndOfLine** is the type for the array that contains the number of characters in each line.

The top-down diagram for the program is

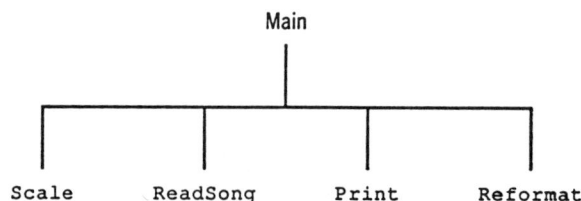

```
                        Main
                          |
        ┌─────────┬───────┴───────┬──────────┐
      Scale    ReadSong         Print     Reformat
```

where

1. Scale, as shown in Figure 15.1a(I), prints the column numbers.
2. ReadSong, as shown in Figure 15.1a(II), reads the text file into the array Screen.
3. Print, as shown in Figure 15.1a(III), prints the contents of the array Screen.
4. Reformat, as shown in Figure 15.1a(IV), reformats the paragraph.

Since Reformat is the only procedure for which we have not written a previous version, let's begin planning it by drawing a top-down diagram

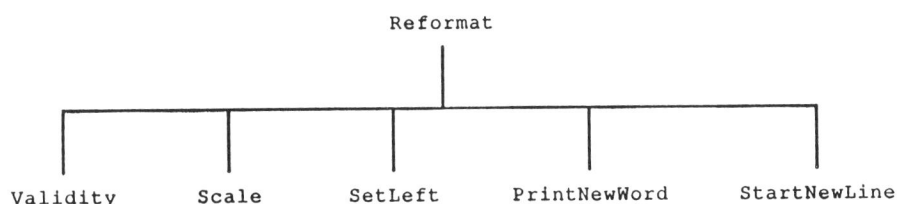

```
                              Reformat
                                 |
      _____|_____
     |          |           |             |                  |
  Validity    Scale      SetLeft      PrintNewWord       StartNewLine
```

where

1. Validity tests whether the left-hand margin read is a smaller number than the right-hand margin.
2. Scale prints the column numbers.
3. SetLeft prints blanks from column 1 through the left-hand margin.
4. PrintNewWord prints a new word.
5. StartNewLine starts printing words on the new line.

Before we write the pseudocode for Reformat, let's analyze how the words in a sentence are reformatted. If we specify columns 12 and 21 for our margins, the first few words of the paragraph appear as follows:

```
           12345678901234567890 1234
                      My country
                      tis of
                      thee,
                      Sweet land
```

The paragraph was written on the file such that a blank separates each word and the last word on a line is immediately followed by a carriage return. As we have seen, ReadSong reads the characters on the file into array Screen. In Reformat, the computer examines the array one character at a time. When the character is not a blank, it is stored in the next element of Letter, the array for the word being formed. When the character is a blank, the computer prints the word just formed.

We will call the number of columns on the reformatted line MaxCol; its value here is 10. When ColCount (the counter for the number of characters in the reformatted line) exceeds MaxCol, the word being formed is printed on the next line. The value of ColCount is increased every time a letter is added to a word and when a blank is appended to each word as it is printed. The table for Figure 15.1a shows how this is done.

The words *My* and *country* are printed on the first line, since the value of `ColCount` is not greater than 10. However, when the string for the next word, *tis*, is complete, the value of `ColCount` is 14. Therefore the computer starts a new line. The value of `ColCount` must be reset before the second word on the new line is processed. Since four columns are allocated to the printing of *tis*, `ColCount` is reset to 4. The process continues in this way, as shown in the table for Figure 15.1a.

Phrase[Column]	Phrase[Column] <> Blank	Letter	Reformatted ColCount	ColCount > MaxColumn	Procedure
M	True	M	1	1 > 10 = False	continue
y	True	My	2	2 > 10 = False	continue
Blank	False		2	2 > 10 = False	print word ColCount:=3
c	True	c	4	4 > 10 = False	continue
.	.	.	.	.	.
.	.	.	.	.	.
y	True	country	10	10 > 10 = False	continue
Blank	False		10	10 > 10 = False	print word ColCount:=11
t	True	t	12	12 > 10 = True	continue
i	True	ti	13	13 > 10 = True	continue
s	True	tis	14	14 > 10 = True	continue
Blank	False		14	14 > 10 = True	Start new line ColCount:= 3 print word ColCount:= 4
o	True	o	5	5 > 10 = False	continue
f	True	of	6	6 > 10 = False	continue

TABLE FOR FIGURE 15.1a. Shows how *My country tis of thee* is handled by the program.

We can now write the pseudocode:

Read left-hand and right-hand margins;
Check for the validity of these numbers;
Set counter for the letters in a word to zero;
Set column # (`ColCount`) for reformatted line to zero;
Calibrate the columns;
Set Left-hand margin
FOR *each line in the unformatted paragraph* DO BEGIN
   Copy unformatted line to array Phrase;
   FOR *each column in unformatted line* DO BEGIN
      IF *the current character is not a blank* THEN BEGIN
         Increment the letter counter
         Copy the current letter into array Letter;
         Increment `ColCount` (for reformatted line)
      END (* IF *);
      IF *end of word* OR *end of line* THEN
         IF `ColCount` > MaxCol THEN BEGIN
         (* *You have exceeded # of columns in reformatted line* *)

Start new line;
Reset column counter for second word on new line
END *(* IF* ColCount **);*
Print new word
END *(* end of word *)*
END *(* FOR each column *)*
END *(* FOR each line *)*

Since the last letter of the last word on a line is reached when Column = NumLetter [LineNum] is true, we write the IF as IF *end of word* OR *end of line* THEN .

IF (Phrase[Column] = Blank) OR (Column = NumLetter[LineNum])THEN BEGIN

The main program is shown in Figure 15.1*b*, and the results of running it are shown in Figure 15.1*c*.

TEST YOURSELF

QUESTION: What is the difference between using Phrase[Column] = Blank (as we do in this program) and NOT (Phrase[Column] IN ['a'..'z', 'A'..'Z') to test for the end of a word?

ANSWER: The former doesn't separate the word from possible punctuation. For instance, *thee*, is treated as a word.

REFORMATTING A PARAGRAPH

```
PROCEDURE Scale; (* produces columns on top of a page *)
VAR Column: integer;
BEGIN
  FOR Column: = 1 TO 80 DO
    write( Column mod 10:1);
  writeln
END (* Scale *);
```

FIGURE 15.1*a*(l). Prints column numbers on top of the screen to enable the reader to see the columns in which the paragraph has been reformatted.

```
TYPE Line = array[1..80] of char;
   Page = array[1..20] of Line;
PROCEDURE ReadSong(VAR Song:text; VAR Screen: Page; VAR LineCount:
LineRange; VAR NumLetter: EndOfLine);
(* Reads a text file into a two-dimensional array *)
VAR Phrase:Line;
   CharCounter: CharRange;

BEGIN (* ReadSong *)
   LineCount:= 0 (* Set Line counter = 0 *);
   WHILE NOT eof(Song) DO BEGIN (* read text into array *)
     CharCounter:= 0 (* Initialize character counter *);
     WHILE NOT eoln(Song) DO BEGIN
       CharCounter:= CharCounter + 1;
       read(Song, Phrase[CharCounter]);
     END (* WHILE NOT eof *);
     readln(Song);
     LineCount:= LineCount + 1;
     NumLetter[LineCount]:= CharCounter ;
     Screen[LineCount]:= Phrase;
   END (* WHILE NOT eoln *)
   close(Song)
END (* ReadSong *);
```

FIGURE 15.1a(II). The same as Figure 11.7a. Reads each character in a line into successive elements of array Phrase and then copies each line to successive elements of Screen.

```
TYPE Line = array[1..80] of char;
  Page = array[1..20] of Line;
  EndOfLine = array[1..20] of integer;
  CharRange = 1..80;
  LineRange = 1..20;
PROCEDURE Print(Screen: Page; LineCount: LineRange; NumLetter: EndOf-
Line);
(* Prints an array *)
VAR Row : LineRange;
  Column: CharRange;
BEGIN
  FOR Row:= 1 TO LineCount DO BEGIN (* Print results *)
    FOR Column:= 1 TO NumLetter[Row] DO
      write( Screen[Row, Column ]);
    writeln
  END (* FOR Row *);
  writeln
END (* Print *);
```

FIGURE 15.1a(III). Prints the unformatted paragraph by copying the two-dimensional array Screen to the screen.

```
PROCEDURE Reformat(Screen: Page; LineCount: LineRange; NumLetter:
EndOfLine);
(* Reformats the paragraph *)
VAR
  Left, Right, MaxColumn, LineNum, Column, ColCount, LetCount: CharRange;
  AtEnd, Valid: boolean;

  Letter, Phrase: Line;
PROCEDURE Validity( MaxColumn:integer; VAR Valid: boolean);
(* If Left is larger than Right, the program stops *)
BEGIN
  IF MaxColumn <= 0 THEN BEGIN
      writeln('MaxColumn is invalid',MaxColumn);
      Valid := false
    END (* THEN *)
  ELSE Valid:= true
END (* Validity *);
PROCEDURE SetLeft(Left:CharRange);
(* Sets the left column of the paragraph *)
BEGIN
  write(Blank:Left − 1)
END (* SetLeft *);
PROCEDURE StartNewLine( VAR ColCount: CharRange; Left, LetCount:
CharRange);
(* Starts a new line *)
BEGIN
  writeln;
  SetLeft(Left); (* Set left margin *)
  (* Reset column counter for second word on new line *)
  ColCount:= LetCount
END (* StartNewLine *);
PROCEDURE PrintNewWord( VAR LetCount: CharRange; Letter: Line);
(* Prints a new word *)
VAR T: CharRange;
BEGIN
  FOR T:= 1 TO LetCount DO
    write( Letter[T] );
  write(Blank);
  LetCount:= 0 (* Reset letter counter for next word *)
END (* PrintNewWord *);
BEGIN (* Reformat *)
  writeln('TYPE Left and Right−hand margins');
  readln( Left, Right);
  MaxColumn:= Right − Left + 1; (* Number of columns in reformatted form *)
  Validity(MaxColumn, Valid);
  LetCount:= 0; (* Letter counter for word *)
  ColCount:= 0; (* Column counter for reformatted line *)
```

```
  IF Valid THEN BEGIN
    Scale;
    SetLeft(Left); (* Set left margin *)
    FOR LineNum:= 1 TO LineCount DO BEGIN
      Phrase:= Screen[LineNum]; (* Copy unformatted line to Phrase *)
      (* FOR each column in original line DO *)
      FOR Column:= 1 TO NumLetter[LineNum] DO BEGIN
        IF Phrase[Column] <> Blank THEN BEGIN
          (* Continue forming the word *)
          LetCount:= LetCount + 1;
          Letter[LetCount]:= Phrase[Column];
          ColCount:= ColCount + 1
        END (* IF *);
      (* IF end of word or end of line THEN *)

      IF (Phrase[Column] = Blank) OR (Column = NumLetter[LineNum])THEN
      BEGIN
        (* Print the word *)
        IF ColCount > MaxColumn THEN
          (* You have exceeded number of columns in reformatted line *)
          StartNewLine(ColCount, Left, LetCount);
        PrintNewWord(LetCount, Letter );
        ColCount:= ColCount + 1 (* because of blank *)
      END (* (Phrase... *)
    END (* FOR Column *);
  END (* FOR LineNum *)
  END (* IF Valid *)
END (* Reformat *);
```

FIGURE 15.1a(IV).   If it is not the end of the word, the procedure copies the letters in the line into array Letter. When the end of the word is encountered, the old word is printed and a new word is started. When the end of the line is encountered, a new line is started and the counters are reinitialized.

```
PROGRAM ArrayPractice(Song, output);
(* Reads Song into an array and then reformats *)
CONST Blank = ' ';
TYPE Line = array[1..80] of char;
  Page = array[1..20] of Line;
  EndOfLine = array[1..20] of integer;
  CharRange = 1..80;
  LineRange = 1..20;
VAR
  Screen: Page;
  LineCount: LineRange;
  NumLetter: EndOfLine;
  Song: text;
```

```
PROCEDURE Scale; (* produces columns on top of a page *)

PROCEDURE Print(Screen: Page; LineCount: LineRange; NumLetter: Endof-
Line);

PROCEDURE Reformat(Screen: Page; LineCount: LineRange; NumLetter:
EndOfLine);

PROCEDURE ReadSong(VAR Song: text; VAR Screen: Page; VAR LineCount:
LineRange; VAR NumLetter: EndOfLine);

BEGIN(* main *)
  reset(Song);
  ReadSong(Song, Screen, LineCount, NumLetter);
  Scale;
  Print(Screen, LineCount, NumLetter);
  Reformat(Screen, LineCount, NumLetter)
END.
```

FIGURE 15.1b. The main program and the headings for the procedures used.

```
12345678901234567890123456789012345678901234567890123456789012345678901234567890
My country tis of thee,
Sweet land of liberty,
Of thee I sing.
Land where my fathers died,
Land of the pilgrims pride,
From every mountain side,
Let freedom ring.

TYPE Left and Right-hand margins
12 40
12345678901234567890123456789012345678901234567890123456789012345678901234567890
            My country tis of thee, Sweet
            land of liberty, Of thee I
            sing. Land where my fathers
            died, Land of the pilgrims
            pride, From every mountain
            side, Let freedom ring.
```

FIGURE 15.1c. Running the program of Figure 15.1b.

15.2

REFORMATTING A PARAGRAPH READ FROM A FILE

BEFORE YOU BEGIN

Have you ever wondered how a word processing program formats a paragraph such that each line starts in, for instance, column 10 and no word in the line extends beyond, let's say, column 70? We now show how this is done. Once we have written and tested the program, we'll alter it so that it also performs a global search and replace.

The next program takes a paragraph written on a text file and reformats it so that the paragraph is written between two specified columns read by the program. For example, if the beginning of the paragraph is

```
My country tis of thee,
Sweet land of liberty,
Of thee I sing.
```

and we specify that the paragraph should appear between columns 12 and 42, then the beginning of the reformatted paragraph appears as follows:

```
12345678901234567890123456789012345678901234567890123456789012345678901234567890
           My country tis of thee, Sweet
           land of liberty, Of thee I
           sing.
```

This includes a calibration of the column numbers so that you can check that the paragraph has been typed between the proper columns. Do you remember the data structures we used in the program that read a text file into a two-dimensional array (Figure 13.7a)

```
TYPE Line = string[80]
     Page = array[1..20] of Line:
```

where Line describes the array into which each line on the file is read and Page describes the array of lines? Since these data structures are appropriate for the present problem, we'll use them here.

The top-down diagram for the program is

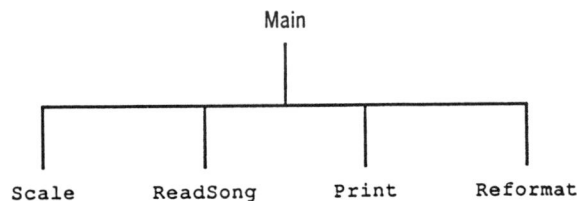

```
                        Main
                          |
        +---------+-------+-------+---------+
        |         |               |         |
      Scale    ReadSong         Print    Reformat
```

where

1. Scale, as shown in Figure 15.1a(I), prints the column numbers.
2. ReadSong, as shown in Figure 15.1a(II), reads the text file into the array Screen.
3. Print, as shown in Figure 15.1a(III), prints the contents of array Screen.
4. Reformat, as shown in Figure 15.1a(IV), reformats the paragraph.

Since Reformat is the only procedure for which we have not written a previous version, let's begin planning it by drawing a top-down diagram

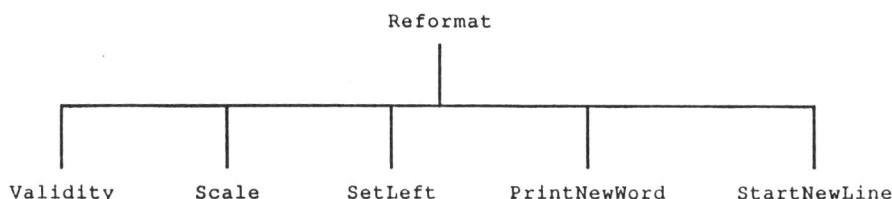

```
                              Reformat
                                 |
   ┌─────────┬──────────┬────────┴───────┬──────────────┐
   |         |          |                |              |
Validity   Scale     SetLeft       PrintNewWord    StartNewLine
```

where

1. Validity tests whether the left-hand margin read is a smaller number than the right-hand margin.
2. Scale prints the column numbers.
3. SetLeft prints blanks from column 1 through the left-hand margin.
4. PrintNewWord prints a new word.
5. StartNewLine starts printing words on the new line.

Before we write the pseudocode for Reformat, let's analyze how the words in a sentence are reformatted. If we specify columns 12 and 21 for our margins, the first few words of the paragraph appear as follows:

```
        12345678901234567890 1234
                   My country
                   tis of
                   thee,
                   Sweet land
```

The paragraph was written on the file such that a blank separates each word and the last word on a line is immediately followed by a carriage return. As we have seen, ReadSong reads the characters on the file into array Screen. In Reformat, the computer examines the array one character at a time. When the character is not a blank, it is stored in the next element of Letter, the string for the word being formed. When the character is a blank, the computer prints the word just formed.

We will call the number of columns on the reformatted line MaxCol; its value here is 10. When ColCount (the counter for the number of characters in the reformatted line) exceeds MaxCol, the word being formed is printed on the next line. The value of ColCount is increased every time a letter is added to a word and when a blank is appended to each word as it is printed. The table for Figure 15.1a shows how this is done.

The words *My* and *country* are printed on the first line. since the value of ColCount is not greater than 10. However, when the string for the next word, *tis*, is complete, the value of ColCount is 14. Therefore the computer starts a new line. The value of ColCount must be reset before the second word on the new line is processed. Since four columns are allocated to the printing of *tis*, Colcount is reset to 4. The process continues in this way, as shown in the table for Figure 15.1a.

Phrase [Column]	Phrase[Column] <> Blank	Letter	Reformatted ColCount	ColCount > MaxColumn	Procedure
M	True	M	1	1 > 10 = False	continue
y	True	My	2	2 > 10 = False	continue
Blank	False		2	2 > 10 = False	print word ColCount:=3
c	True	c	4	4 > 10 = False	continue
.	.	.	.	.	.
.	.		.	.	.
y	True	country	10	10 > 10 = False	continue
Blank	False		10	10 > 10 = False	print word ColCount:=11
t	True	t	12	12 > 10 = True	continue
i	True	ti	13	13 > 10 = True	continue
s	True	tis	14	14 > 10 = True	continue
Blank	False		14	14 > 10 = True	Start new line ColCount: = 3 print word ColCount: = 4
o	True	o	5	5 > 10 = False	continue
f	True	of	6	6 > 10 = False	continue

TABLE FOR FIGURE 15.1a. Show how *My country tis of thee* is handled by the program.

We can now write the pseudocode:

> *Read left-hand and right-hand margins:*
> *Check for the validity of these numbers:*
> *Set counter for the letters in a word to zero:*
> *Set column # (ColCount) for reformatted line to zero:*
> *Calibrate the columns:*
> *Set Left-hand margin:*
> FOR *each line in the unformatted paragraph* DO BEGIN
>   *Copy unformatted line to array* Phrase:
>   FOR *each column in unformatted line* DO BEGIN
>   IF *the current character is not a blank* THEN BEGIN
>   *Increment the letter counter*
>   *Add the current letter to* Letter:
>   *Increment* ColCount *(for reformatted line)*
>   END {IF}:
>   IF *end of word* OR *end of line* THEN
>   IF ColCount > MaxCol THEN BEGIN
>   {*You have exceeded # of columns in reformatted line*}

> *Start new line;*
> *Reset column counter for second word on new line*
> END *(* IF ColCount *)*;
> *Print new word*
> END *(* end of word *)*
> END *(* FOR each column *)*
> END *(* FOR each line *)*

Since the last letter of the last word on a line is reached when Column = NumLetter [LineNum] is true, we write the IF as IF *end of word* OR *end of line* THEN.

IF (Phrase[Column] = Blank) OR (Column = NumLetter[LineNum])THEN BEGIN

We translate *Add the current letter to* Letter to

Letter:= Letter + Phrase[Column]

where we concatenate the current letter, Phrase[Column], with the string Letter. For instance, if Phrase[Column] is s and Letter is originally ti, the final value of Letter will be tis.

The main program is shown in Figure 15.1*b*, and the results of running it are shown in Figure 15.1*c*.

TEST YOURSELF

QUESTION: What is the difference between using Phrase[Column] = Blank (as we do in this program) and NOT (Phrase[Column] IN ['a'..'z', 'A'..'Z']) to test for the end of a word?

ANSWER: The former doesn't separate the word from possible punctuation. For instance, *thee,* is treated as a word.

Adding Search and Replace to the Reformatting

Before we write a program that performs a search and replace as well as reformats a paragraph, let's convert all the procedures of the last program into a unit called Format, shown in Figure 15.1*d* (we will also use unit Search [Figure 11.12*a*] to perform the search and replace). The following declarations that will be used by the host program are placed in the interface section of Format:

TYPE Page = array[1..20] of Line;
LineRange = 0..20;
VAR Screen: Page;
LineCount: LineRange;
Song: text;
Row:LineRange

52

We will show that we can't define Line = string[80] here. It is, however, defined in Search. Therefore, we must start the interface section of Format with USES Search so that Format can refer to the definition of Line there.

The present program is similar to the host program of Figure 9.11 that performed a search and replace for one line only, using the procedure with the heading

```
PROCEDURE Replace(New_Word, Old_Word :Line; VAR Sentence:Line);
```

In order to perform this process for all the lines in the file, we now write

```
FOR Row: = 1 TO LineCount DO
    Replace(New_Word, Old_Word, Screen[Row]);
```

as shown in Figure 15.1e. The array Screen is declared in VAR Screen: Page in unit Format, and its type is also defined there in Page = ARRAY[1..20] OF Line. Thus the type of the actual parameter Screen[Row] is Line. Why can't we define Line in Format? The answer is that in unit Search the corresponding formal parameter, Sentence, is given in

```
PROCEDURE Replace(New_Word, Old_Word :Line; VAR Sentence:Line);
```

and its type (Line) is defined in Search. The type of both the formal parameter and the corresponding actual parameter must be defined in the same definition. If Line is defined in Format as well as in Search, Turbo Pascal assumes that since the type of Screen is given in Page = ARRAY[1..20] OF Line in unit Format, the definition of Screen[Row], namely, Line, is given there as well. Consequently the type of the actual parameter wouldn't be defined in the same statement with the type of the corresponding formal parameter, and a *type mismatch* error would result. Note that normally we can place the same definition in many units. The running of the program is shown in Figure 15.1f.

TEST YOURSELF

QUESTION: If the actual parameter in Replace were Phrase of type Line, could you define Line in both units?

ANSWER: Yes, if Phrase is declared in both Search and Format. If you declare it only in Format, you'll get a type mismatch error because Turbo Pascal would then assume that its type is defined in the same unit.

REFORMATTING A PARAGRAPH

```
PROCEDURE Scale; {produces columns on top of a page}
VAR Column: integer;
BEGIN
    FOR Column: = 1 TO 80 DO
        write( Column mod 10:1);
    writeln
END {Scale};
```

FIGURE 15.1a(I). Prints column numbers on top of the screen to enable the reader to see the columns in which the paragraph has been reformatted.

```
USES crt;
CONST Blank = ' ';
   Null = '';
TYPE Line = string[80];
   Page = array[1..20] of Line;
   EndOfLine = array[1..20] of integer;
   CharRange = 0..80;
   LineRange = 0..20;
PROCEDURE ReadSong(VAR Song: text; VAR Screen: Page; VAR LineCount:
LineRange);
{Reads a text file into a two-dimensional array}
VAR Phrase:Line;
BEGIN {ReadSong}
   LineCount: = 0 {Set Line counter = 0};
   WHILE NOT eof(Song) DO BEGIN {read text into an array}
     LineCount: = LineCount + 1;
     readln(Song,Screen[LineCount]);
   END {WHILE NOT eoln}
END {ReadSong};
```

FIGURE 15.1a(II).   The same as Figure 11.7a. Reads each character in a line into successive elements of array Phrase and then copies each line into successive elements of Screen.

```
PROCEDURE Print(Screen: Page; LineCount: LineRange);
{Prints an array}
     VAR Row :LineRange;
     BEGIN
       FOR Row: = 1 TO LineCount DO {Print results}
           writeln(Screen[Row]);
     END {Print};
```

FIGURE 15.1a(III).   Prints the unformatted paragraph by copying the two-dimensional array Screen to the screen.

```
PROCEDURE Reformat(Screen: Page; LineCount: LineRange);
{Reformats the paragraph}
VAR
   Left, Right, MaxColumn, LineNum, Column, ColCount, LetCount: CharRange;
   AtEnd, Valid: boolean;
   Letter, Phrase: Line;
PROCEDURE Validity( MaxColumn:integer; VAR Valid: boolean);
{If Left is larger than Right, the program stops
BEGIN
   IF MaxColumn <= 0 THEN BEGIN
       writeln('MaxColumn is invalid',MaxColumn);
       Valid := false
     END {THEN}
```

```
      ELSE Valid: = true
END {Validity};

PROCEDURE SetLeft(Left:CharRange);
{Sets the left column of the paragraph}
BEGIN
   write(Blank:Left - 1)
END {SetLeft};

PROCEDURE StartNewLine( VAR ColCount: CharRange; Left, LetCount:
CharRange);
{Starts a new line}
BEGIN
   writeln;
   SetLeft(Left); {Set Left margin}
   {Reset column counter for second word on new line}
   ColCount: = LetCount
END {StartNewLine};

PROCEDURE PrintNewWord( VAR LetCount: CharRange; VAR Letter: Line);
{Prints a new word}
BEGIN
   write(Letter);
   write(Blank);
   LetCount: = 0;
   Letter: = Null; {reset letter string for next word}
END {PrintNewWord};

BEGIN {Reformat}
   writeln('TYPE Left and Right-hand margins');
   readln( Left, Right);
   MaxColumn: = Right - Left + 1; {Number of columns in reformatted form}
   Validity(MaxColumn, Valid);
   LetCount: = 0; {Letter counter for word}
   ColCount: = 0; {Column counter for reformatted line}
   Letter: = Null;
   IF Valid THEN BEGIN
      Scale;
SetLeft(Left); {Set Left margin}
FOR LineNum: = 1 TO LineCount DO BEGIN
   Phrase: = Screen[LineNum]; {Copy unformatted line to Phrase}
   {FOR each column in original line DO}
   FOR Column: = 1 TO Length(Phrase) DO BEGIN
      IF Phrase[Column] <> Blank THEN BEGIN
         {Continue forming the word}
         LetCount: = LetCount + 1;
         Letter: = Letter + Phrase[Column];
         ColCount: = ColCount + 1
      END {IF};
```

```
        {IF end of word or end of line THEN}
      IF (Phrase[Column] = Blank) OR (Column = Length(Phrase))THEN BEGIN
        {Print the word}
        IF ColCount > MaxColumn THEN
          {You have exceeded number of columns in reformatted line}
          StartNewLine(ColCount, Left, LetCount);
        PrintNewWord(LetCount, Letter );
        ColCount:= ColCount + 1 {because of blank}
      END {(Phrase...}
    END {FOR Column};
  END {FOR LineNum}
END{IF Valid}
END {Reformat};
```

FIGURE 15.1a(IV). If it is not the end of the word, the letters in the line are concatenated with the string Letter. When the end of the word is encountered, the old word is printed and a new word is started. When the end of the line is encountered, a new line is started, the counters are reinitialized, and Letter is set to the null string.

```
PROGRAM ArrayPractice;
{Reads a song into an array and then reformats}
USES crt;
CONST Blank = ' ';
  Null = '';
TYPE Line = string[80];
  Page = array[1..20] of Line;
  EndOfLine = array[1..20] of integer;
  CharRange = 0..80;
  LineRange = 0..20;
VAR
  Screen: Page;
  LineCount: LineRange;
  NumLetter: EndOfLine;
  Song: text;
PROCEDURE Scale; {produces columns on top of the page}
PROCEDURE Print(Screen: Page; LineCount: LineRange);
PROCEDURE Reformat(Screen: Page; LineCount: LineRange);
PROCEDURE ReadSong(VAR Song:text; VAR Screen: Page; VAR LineCount:
LineRange);
BEGIN{main}
  clrscr;
  assign(Song, 'country.txt');
  reset(Song); .
  ReadSong(Song, Screen, LineCount);
```

```
        Scale;
        Print(Screen, LineCount);
        Reformat(Screen, LineCount)
     END.
```

FIGURE 15.1b.   The main program and the headings for the procedures used.

```
1234567890123456789012345678901234567890123456789012345678901234567890123456789
My country tis of thee,
Sweet land of liberty,
Of thee I sing.
Land where my fathers died,
Land of the pilgrims pride,
From every mountain side,
Let freedom ring.
TYPE Left and Right-hand margins
12 40
1234567890123456789012345678901234567890123456789012345678901234567890123456789
            My country tis of thee, Sweet
            land of liberty, Of thee I
            sing. Land where my fathers
            died, Land of the pilgrims
            pride, From every mountain
            side, Let freedom ring.
```

FIGURE 15.1c.   Running the program of Figure 15.1b.

REFORMATTING AND GLOBAL SEARCH AND REPLACE

```
UNIT Format;
{Reads a song into an array and then reformats}
INTERFACE
USES Search;

TYPE Page = array[1..20] of Line;
   LineRange = 0..20;
VAR
   Screen: Page;
   LineCount: LineRange;
   Song: text;
   Row:LineRange;

PROCEDURE Print(Screen: Page; LineCount: LineRange);

PROCEDURE Reformat(Screen: Page; LineCount: LineRange);

PROCEDURE ReadSong(VAR Song:text; VAR Screen: Page;
         VAR LineCount: LineRange);

IMPLEMENTATION
CONST Blank = ' ';
   Null = '';
TYPE
   CharRange = 0..80;

{Insert all the procedures from the previous programs}
END. {UNIT Format}
```

FIGURE 15.1d. The UNIT Format reads a paragraph into an array and then reformats it.

```
PROGRAM ArrayPractice;
{Performs global search and replace, then reformats}
{Makes use of units}
USES crt, Format. Search;
BEGIN{main}
  clrscr;
  assign(Song, 'country.txt');
  reset(Song);
  ReadSong(Song, Screen, LineCount);
  Print(Screen, LineCount);
  writeln;
  write('Type the word to be replaced:');
  readln(Old_Word);
  write('Type new Word:');
  readln(New_Word);
  {Replace the lowercase word}
  FOR Row:= 1 TO LineCount DO
    Replace(New_Word, Old_Word, Screen[Row]);
  {Replace the capitalized word}
  Old_Word:= Capitalized(Old_Word);
  New_Word:= Capitalized(New_Word);
  writeln;
  FOR Row:= 1 TO LineCount DO
  Replace(New_Word, Old_Word, Screen[Row]);
  Reformat(Screen, LineCount)
END.
```

FIGURE 15.1e.   Performs a global search and replace and then reformats.

```
My country tis of thee,
Sweet land of liberty,
Of thee I sing.
Land where my fathers died,
Land of the pilgrims pride,
From every mountain side,
Let freedom ring.

Type the word to be replaced:thee
Type new Word:you

TYPE Left and Right-hand margins
20 40
12345678901234567890123456789012345678901234567890123456789012345678901234567890
                         My country tis of
                         you, Sweet land of
                         liberty, Of you I
                         sing. Land where my
                         fathers died, Land of
                         the pilgrims pride,
                         From every mountain
                         side, Let freedom
                         ring.
```

FIGURE 15.1f. Running the program of Figure 15.1e. The word "you" has replaced "thee."

11.3

MAKING AN INDEX FOR LAST NAMES IN A PARAGRAPH

BEFORE YOU BEGIN

Have you ever wondered how an author index in the back of a textbook is produced? The following discussion shows how a simplified model would be written.

Let's write a program that will find all the last names of married women in a paragraph stored on a file and on which line they were found. For instance, in

```
Hello Mrs. Smith, Mrs. Jones, and Mrs.
Abrams. Lend me your ears. How are
Mrs. Davis; and Mrs. Cook?
```

the last names of the married women appearing on the first line are "Smith" and "Jones". We'll write the program in four steps:

Step 1 finds the word (here, the last name) immediately following the first occurrence of "Mrs." in a sentence, assuming that the delimiter for this word is a blank. Thus given "Hello Mrs. Smith; and Mrs. Jones? Do you know Mrs. Abrams", the program would find "Smith;". In other words, the punctuation is included in the word.

Step 2 finds all the last names in a sentence (again, assuming that a blank is the delimiter). Thus in the sentence of Step 1, it would find "Smith;" and "Jones?", but not "Abrams" because "Abrams" is immediately followed by a carriage return. Again, the punctuation marks are included in the names found.

Step 3 finds all the last names in a sentence (assuming that any nonletter is a delimiter). Thus it would find "Smith", "Jones", and "Abrams".

Step 4 extends Step 3 to a paragraph. In addition, when a sentence ends with "Mrs.", the program will print the first word in the next sentence.

Step 1
The pseudocode for Step 1 is

> *Read* LeadWord;
> *Read sentence from the file;*
> *Find and print the word after* LeadWord

where in our case LeadWord is "Mrs.". This suggests the top-down diagram shown in Figure 11.7a, where LeadWord in our case is 'Mrs.". The pseudocode for procedure Finds is

> *Find the position of* LeadWord *in the sentence;*
> *Redefine the sentence so that the part from its beginning*
> *to the end of* LeadWord *is erased.*
> *Find the end of the first word in the redefined sentence;*
> *Copy that word to the printer.*

This is translated into procedure Finds, shown in Figure 11.7b(I), where the value of Position is the position of the beginning of LeadWord in the sentence and the value of PosNextWord is the position of the beginning of the next word. To see how this works, let's examine the following: If, for instance, the original contents of Sentence are

H	e	l	l	o		M	r	s	.		S	m	i	t	h	;		a	n	d		M	r	s	.		J	o	n	e	s	?	
1	2	3	4	5	6	7	8	9	10	11	12	13	14	15	16	17	18	19	10	11	12	13	14	15	16	17	18	19	10	11	12	13	14

the value of Position is 7, the value of PosNextWord is 12, and thus Copy(Sentence, Rest, PosNextWord, ToEnd) becomes Copy(Sentence, Rest, 7, 300). We use 300 here to simplify the evaluation, since only the part of the string up to its end is copied. The redefined sentence, Rest, becomes

S	m	i	t	h	;		a	n	d		M	r	s	.		J	o	n	e	s	?
1	2	3	4	5	6	7	8	9	10	11	12	13	14	15	16	17	18	19	10	11	12

We implement *Find the end of the first word* by subtracting 1 from the position of the next blank, as shown in function EndWord in Figure 11.7b(II). The value of this position, 6, is assigned to EndPosition. Thus Copy(Rest, TargetWord, 1, EndPosition) becomes Copy(Rest, TargetWord, 1, 6) and "Smith;" is assigned to TargetWord.

TEST YOURSELF

QUESTION: Why can't we find the position of the next blank by writing EndWord := Pos(Blank, Sentence) − 1 in function EndWord?

ANSWER: Since the type of both parameters must be Line, a type mismatch will occur because Blank is a constant.

Procedure Readfile has already been displayed in Figure 11.3d(I), but now it reads a different file. The main program and the headings for the procedures are shown in Figure 11.7c, and the running of the program is shown in Figure 11.7d.

Step II

In order to find the words that follows each occurrence of LeadWord, let's rewrite procedure Finds. The pseudocode for the new version is

Find the position of LeadWord *in the sentence;*
WHILE *that position* <> *0* DO BEGIN
    Redefine the sentence so that the part from its beginning
    to the end of LeadWord *is erased.*
    Find the end of the first word in the redefined sentence;
    Copy that word to the printer;
    Find the position of LeadWord *in the redefined sentence*
END (* WHILE *);

In order to search for each occurrence of LeadWord, change Copy(Sentence, Rest, PosNextWord, ToEnd) in the previous version of procedure Finds to

    Copy(Sentence, Sentence, PosNextWord, ToEnd);

as shown in Figure 11.8a. Redefining Sentence this way erases the sentence up to the word following LeadWord and allows the program in

    Copy(Sentence, TargetWord, 1, EndPosition);

to search for a new last name each time the loop is executed. as shown in the table for Figure 11.8a, where EndPosition indicates the end of the first word. The main program is shown in Figure 11.8b.

Step III

What's new here is that function EndWord is rewritten so that when it finds the end of the first word in the redefined Sentence. it looks for any nonletter as the delimiter. Its pseudocode is

> *Set* Index *to 1;*
> WHILE *the current character is a letter* DO
>   *Increment* Index *by 1;*
> *Since the last value of* Index *is for a nonletter,*
> *subtract 1 from* Index

Because the boolean expression in the translation of the WHILE includes AND (Index <= Length(Sentence), as shown in Figure 11.9a, the function finds the last word in the sentence even if it is immediately followed by a carriage return. The results of running the program are shown in Figure 11.9b.

Step IV

This step extends Step III to a program that reads a paragraph. In order to find a last name (TargetWord) even if "Mrs." is the last word in the preceding sentence. do the following:

1. Alter procedure Finds so that it tests whether LeadWord is the last word in the sentence: this means that TargetWord will be the first word in the next sentence. If it is, set the boolean VAR parameter, NextSentence, to true in this procedure, as shown in Figure 11.10a(I):

        IF PosNextWord >= length(Sentence) THEN
          NextSentence: = True;

2. Add procedure FirstWord. which prints the first word in the sentence: see Figure 11.10a(II). This will be activated if the value of NextSentence is True.

3. Add procedure ReadParag, Figure 11.10a(III). so that you can see the paragraph before you make any alterations.

4. Add procedure ReadFile. Figure 11.10a(IV). which reads each line of the paragraph. If the previous line ends with LeadWord. this procedure will direct the computer to print the first word in the next line.

The top-down diagram for the program is

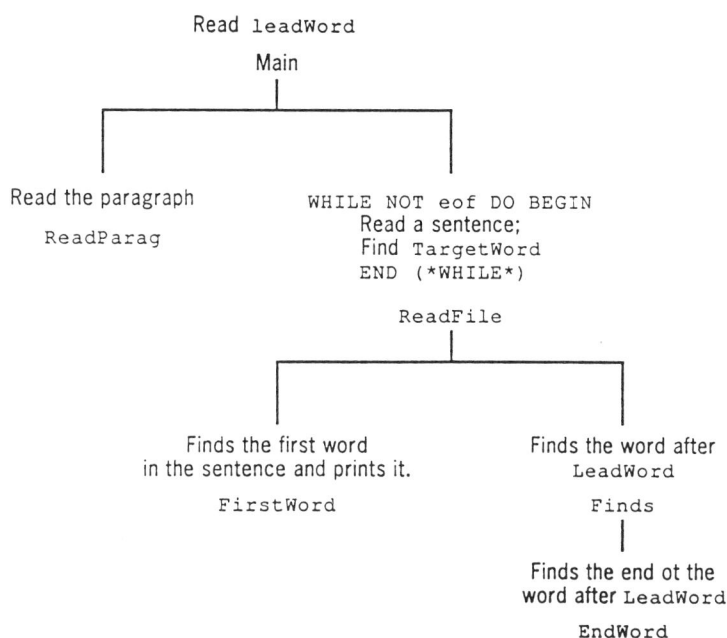

```
                    Read leadWord
                        Main
                          |
        _____
        |                                        |
  Read the paragraph          WHILE NOT eof DO BEGIN
                                Read a sentence;
     ReadParag                  Find TargetWord
                              END (*WHILE*)

                                 ReadFile
                                    |
                    _____
                    |                              |
          Finds the first word          Finds the word after
          in the sentence and prints it.      LeadWord

               FirstWord                      Finds
                                                |
                                      Finds the end ot the
                                      word after LeadWord

                                          EndWord
```

Figure 11.10*b* displays the main program, the include file references, and the headings for the procedures used that are not include files. Finally, the program is run in Figure 11.10*c*. The output displays the line number and the last names occurring on the line with that number. If you arrange this information in alphabetic order, you can construct an index.

TEST YOURSELF

QUESTION: The statement part of procedure ReadFile is

```
BEGIN
  reset(ParagFile);
  NextSentence:= False;
  N:=0;
  WHILE NOT eof(ParagFile) DO BEGIN
    N:= N + 1;
    readln(ParagFile, Sentence);
    writeln('Sentence #', N, ':', Sentence);
    writeln('The words following ', LeadWord, ' are:');
    IF NextSentence THEN BEGIN
      FirstWord(Sentence);
      NextSentence:= False
    END (* IF *);
    Finds(LeadWord, Sentence, NextSentence)
  END (* WHILE NOT eof *);
END (* ReadFile *);
```

a. What happens if you exclude the NextSentence := False that precedes the IF?

b. What happens if you exclude the NextSentence := False that follows the IF?

c. What happens if you place the IF after the activation of Finds instead of before it?

ANSWER:

a. Since NextSentence may be true, the program will print the first word on the first line.

b. When NextSentence is true, not only will the first word of the next sentence be printed, but also the first word of the sentence after that sentence.

c. Since the first sentence ends with "Mrs.", the value of NextSentence will be true. Because the IF follows, the program will print the first word of the first sentence instead of the first word of the second sentence.

FORMING AN INDEX
STEP I: FINDS THE WORD AFTER A GIVEN WORD

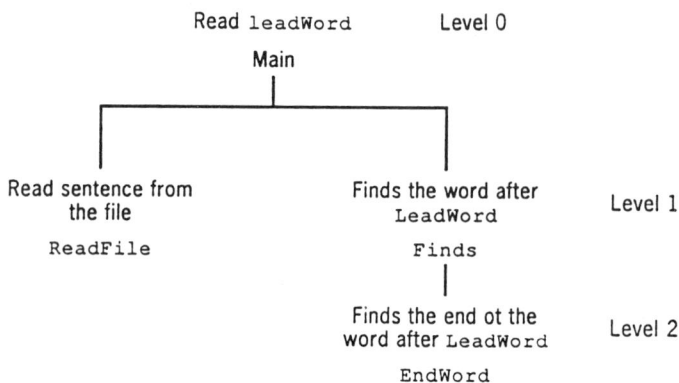

FIGURE 11.7a. The top-down diagram for a program that finds a word in a sentence following another word (called LeadWord) that is read into the program.

```
CONST Blank = ' ';
   ToEnd = 300;
   Max = 126;
TYPE Line = ARRAY[0..Max] OF Char;
PROCEDURE Finds(LeadWord :Line; VAR Sentence:Line);
(* Finds the word after LeadWord *)
VAR Rest, TargetWord:Line;
   EndPosition, Position, PosNextWord, WordLength:integer;
BEGIN
   Position:= Pos(LeadWord, Sentence);
   WordLength:= length(LeadWord) + 1;
   (* ...Eliminate LeadWord from sentence *)
   PosNextWord:= Position + WordLength;
   Copy(Sentence, Rest, PosNextWord, ToEnd);
   writeln('The rest of the sentence is :');
   Print(Rest);
   writeln;
   (* ...Find the end of the next word *)
   EndPosition:= EndWord(Rest);
   Copy(Rest, TargetWord, 1, EndPosition);
   write('The next word is ');
   Print(TargetWord);
   writeln
END; (* Finds *)
```

FIGURE 11.7b(I).   Finds the word after LeadWord by copying the part of the sentence following LeadWord to Rest and then printing the first word in Rest.

```
FUNCTION EndWord(Sentence:Line):integer;
(* Finds the end of the next word in a sentence *)
VAR OneBlank:Line;
BEGIN
   OneBlank[1]:= Blank;
   OneBlank[0]:= chr(1);
   EndWord:= Pos(OneBlank, Sentence) - 1
END (* EndWord *);
```

FIGURE 11.7b(II).   Finds the end of the first word in a sentence. The delimiter is a blank.

```
PROGRAM Replacement(input, output, ParagFile);
(* Finds the word after the inputted word *)
CONST Blank = ' ';
   ToEnd = 300;
   Max = 126;
TYPE Line = ARRAY[0..Max] OF Char;
VAR LeadWord, Sentence:Line;
   EndPosition, Position:integer;
   ParagFile:text;
FUNCTION EndWord(Sentence:Line):integer;
PROCEDURE Finds(LeadWord:Line; VAR Sentence:Line);
PROCEDURE ReadFile(VAR Sentence: Line);
BEGIN
   ReadFile(Sentence);
   writeln;
   writeln('Type the word preceding the desired word');
   ReadString(input, LeadWord);
   Finds(LeadWord, Sentence)
END.
```

FIGURE 11.7c.   Shows the main program and the headings of the procedures used. The sentence read is on a file called ParagFile.

```
The sentence read was:
Hello Mrs. Smith; and Mrs. Jones? Do you know Mrs. Abrams
Type the word preceding the desired word
Mrs.
The rest of the sentence is :
Smith; and Mrs. Jones? Do you know Mrs. Abrams
The next word is Smith;
```

FIGURE 11.7d.   Running the program of Figure 11.7c. Since the delimiter is a blank, the punctuation immediately following the word is also included.

FORMING AN INDEX
STEP II: FINDS THE WORD AFTER EACH OCCURRENCE OF A GIVEN WORD

```pascal
PROGRAM Replacement(input, output, ParagFile);
(* Extracts all occurrences of words that follow a target
substring in a string. The words must be terminated by blanks. *)
CONST Blank = ' ';
  ToEnd = 300;
  Max = 126;
TYPE Line = ARRAY[0..Max] OF Char;
VAR TargetWord, LeadWord, Sentence:Line;
  ParagFile:text;
PROCEDURE ReadFile(VAR Sentence: Line);
FUNCTION EndWord(Sentence:Line):integer;
PROCEDURE Finds(LeadWord, Sentence:Line);
(* Finds all the words that follow a substring *)
VAR EndPosition, PosNextWord, WordLength, Position:word;
  TargetWord:Line;
BEGIN
  WordLength:= length(LeadWord) + 1;
  Position:= Pos(LeadWord, Sentence);
  write('The words to the right of each ');
  Print(LeadWord);
  writeln(' are:');
  WHILE Position <> 0 DO BEGIN
    (* ...Eliminate LeadWord from sentence *)
    PosNextWord:= Position + WordLength;
    Copy(Sentence, Sentence, PosNextWord, ToEnd);
    (* ...Find the ending of the next word *)
    EndPosition:= EndWord(Sentence);
    Copy(Sentence, TargetWord, 1, EndPosition);
    Print(TargetWord);
    writeln;
    (* ...Find next position of LeadWord *)
    Position:= Pos(LeadWord, Sentence)
  END (* WHILE *)
END; (* Finds *)
BEGIN
  ReadFile(Sentence);
  writeln;
  writeln('Type the word preceding the desired word');
  ReadString(input, LeadWord);
  Finds(LeadWord, Sentence)
END.
```

FIGURE 11.8a. Finds the word (including the possible punctuation following it) that follows each occurrence of LeadWord in the sentence by continually redefining the sentence as beginning after the last occurrence of LeadWord found.

Sentence on left-hand side of Copy	TargetWord
Smith; and Mrs. Jones? Do you know Mrs. Abrams	Smith;
Jones? Do you know Mrs. Abrams	Jones?
Abrams	Abrams

TABLE FOR FIGURE 11.8a. Each time Copy(Sentence, Sentence, PosNext-Word, ToEnd) is executed, the value of Sentence is changed, and so is that of TargetWord.

```
The sentence read was:
Hello Mrs. Smith; and Mrs. Jones? Do you know Mrs. Abrams
Type the word preceding the desired word
Mrs.
The words to the right of each Mrs. are:
Smith;
Jones?
```

FIGURE 11.8b. Running the program of Figure 11.8a. The program doesn't find "Abrams", since it is terminated by a carriage return. We correct for this in the next program.

FORMING AN INDEX
STEP III: FINDS THE WORD AFTER EACH OCCURRENCE OF A GIVEN WORD EVEN IF THE WORD ENDS WITH A CARRIAGE RETURN

```
PROGRAM Replacement(input, output, ParagFile);
(* Extracts all occurrences of words that follow a target
substring in a string. The words are terminated by any
punctuation or end-of line mark *)
CONST Blank = ' ';
  ToEnd = 300;
  Max = 126;
TYPE Line = ARRAY[0..Max] OF Char;
VAR TargetWord, LeadWord, Sentence:Line;
  ParagFile:text;
FUNCTION EndWord(Sentence:Line):integer;
(* Finds the end of the next word in a sentence *)
VAR Index:integer;
BEGIN
  Index:= 1;
  WHILE (Sentence[Index] IN ['a'..'z', 'A'..'Z'])
    AND (Index <= Length(Sentence) ) DO
      Index:= Index + 1;
  EndWord:= Index - 1
END (* EndWord *);
PROCEDURE ReadFile(VAR Sentence: Line);
PROCEDURE Finds(LeadWord, Sentence:Line);
BEGIN
```

```
        ReadFile(Sentence);
        writeln;
        writeln('Type the word preceding the desired word');
        ReadString(input, LeadWord);
        Finds(LeadWord, Sentence)
    END.
```

FIGURE 11.9a.   Finds the word (excluding possible punctuation) that follows each occurrence of LeadWord in the sentence by continually redefining the sentence as beginning after the last occurrence of LeadWord found. To detect a word terminated by a carriage return and not by punctuation, we include an additional test.

```
    The sentence read was:
    Hello Mrs. Smith; and Mrs. Jones? Do you know Mrs. Abrams
    Type the word preceding the desired word
    Mrs.
    The words to the right of each Mrs. are:
    Smith
    Jones
    Abrams
```

FIGURE 11.9b.   Running the program of Figure 11.9a.

FORMING AN INDEX
STEP IV: FINDS THE WORD AFTER EACH OCCURRENCE OF A GIVEN WORD EVEN IF THE WORD ENDS WITH A CARRIAGE RETURN OR OCCURS AS THE FIRST WORD IN THE NEXT SENTENCE

```
    PROCEDURE Finds(LeadWord, Sentence:Line;
            VAR NextSentence:boolean);
    (* ...Finds all the words that follow a substring *)
    VAR EndPosition, PosNextWord, WordLength, Position:word;
      TargetWord:Line;
    BEGIN
      WordLength:= length(LeadWord) + 1;
      Position:= Pos(LeadWord, Sentence);
      WHILE Position <> 0 DO BEGIN
        (* ...Eliminate LeadWord from sentence *)
        PosNextWord:= Position + WordLength;
        IF PosNextWord >= length(Sentence) THEN
          NextSentence:= True;
        Copy(Sentence, Sentence, PosNextWord, ToEnd);
        (* Find the ending of the next word *)
        EndPosition:= EndWord(Sentence);
        Copy(Sentence, TargetWord, 1, EndPosition);
        Print(TargetWord);
        writeln;
```

```
        Position:= Pos(LeadWord, Sentence)
     END (* WHILE *)
  END; (* Finds *)
```

FIGURE 11.10a(I).   The procedure of Figure 11.8a rewritten so that it detects if the word following the substring occurs on the next line.

```
     PROCEDURE FirstWord(Sentence:Line);
     (* ...If the previous LeadWord was at end of last sentence,
     ... this finds first word *)
     VAR EndPosition:word;
       TargetWord:Line;
     BEGIN
       EndPosition:= EndWord(Sentence);
       Copy(Sentence, TargetWord, 1, EndPosition);
       Print(TargetWord);
       writeln
     END (* FirstWord *);
```

FIGURE 11.10a(II).   If the previous LeadWord was at the end of the last sentence, this procedure finds the first word in the current sentence.

```
     PROCEDURE ReadParagraph(VAR ParagFile:text);
     (* Reads a paragraph from a file *)
     VAR Sentence:Line;
     BEGIN
       reset(ParagFile);
       writeln('The paragraph read was:');
       writeln;
       WHILE NOT eof(ParagFile) DO BEGIN
         ReadString(ParagFile, Sentence);
         readln(ParagFile);
         Print(Sentence);
         writeln;
       END(* WHILE NOT eof *);
       writeln
     END (* ReadParagraph *);
```

FIGURE 11.10a(III).   Reads a paragraph from a file.

```
PROCEDURE ReadFile(LeadWord:Line);
(* Reads a sentence from a file *)
VAR NextSentence:boolean;
   N:integer;
BEGIN
  reset(ParagFile);
  NextSentence:= False;
  N:=0;
  WHILE NOT eof(ParagFile) DO BEGIN
    N:= N + 1;
    ReadString(ParagFile, Sentence);
    readln(ParagFile); (* Doesn't work if in ReadString *)
    writeln;
    write('Sentence #', N, ':');
    Print( Sentence);
    writeln;
    write('The words following ');
    Print(LeadWord);
    writeln(' are:');
    IF NextSentence THEN BEGIN
       FirstWord(Sentence);
       NextSentence:= False
    END (* IF *);
    Finds(LeadWord, Sentence, NextSentence)
  END (* WHILE NOT eof *);
END (* ReadFile *);
```

FIGURE 11.10a(IV).   Finds all the target words in the paragraph.

```
PROGRAM Search(input, output, ParagFile);
(* ...Prints all occurrences of words in a file that follows
...a target substring in a string. The words are terminated
...by any punctuation or end-of line mark. The file consists
...of a paragraph *)
CONST Blank = ' ';
  ToEnd = 300;
  Max = 126;
TYPE Line = ARRAY[0..Max] OF char;
VAR TargetWord, LeadWord :Line;
  ParagFile:text;
FUNCTION EndWord(Sentence:Line):integer;
PROCEDURE FirstWord(Sentence:Line);
PROCEDURE Finds(LeadWord, Sentence:Line; VAR NextSentence:boolean);
PROCEDURE ReadParagraph(VAR ParagFile:text);
PROCEDURE ReadFile(VAR ParagFile:text; LeadWord:Line);
BEGIN
  ReadParagraph(ParagFile);
  writeln('Type the word preceding the desired word');
  ReadString(Input, LeadWord);
  ReadFile(LeadWord)
END.
```

FIGURE 11.10b. The main program and the headings of the procedures it uses.

```
The paragraph read was:
Hello Mrs. Smith, Mrs. Jones, and Mrs.
Abrams. Lend me your ears. How are
Mrs. Davis; and Mrs. Cook?
Type the word preceding the desired word
Mrs.
Sentence #1:Hello Mrs. Smith, Mrs. Jones, and Mrs.
The words following Mrs. are:
Smith
Jones
Sentence #2:Abrams. Lend me your ears. How are
The words following Mrs. are:
Abrams
Sentence #3:Mrs. Davis; and Mrs. Cook?
The words following Mrs. are:
Davis
Cook
```

FIGURE 11.10c. Running the program of Figure 11.10a.

11.3

MAKING AN INDEX FOR LAST NAMES IN A PARAGRAPH

BEFORE YOU BEGIN

Have you ever wondered how an author index in the back of a textbook is produced? The following discussion shows how a simplified model would be written.

Let's write a program that will find all the last names of married women in a paragraph stored on a file and on which line they were found. For instance, in

```
Hello Mrs. Smith, Mrs. Jones, and Mrs.
Abrams. Lend me your ears. How are
Mrs. Davis; and Mrs. Cook?
```

the last names of the married women appearing on the first line are "Smith" and "Jones". We'll write the program in four steps:

Step 1 finds the word (last name) immediately following the first occurence of "Mrs." in a sentence. assuming that the delimiter for this word is a blank. Thus given "Hello Mrs. Smith: and Mrs. Jones? Do you know Mrs. Abrams", the program would find "Smith:".

Step 2 finds all the last names in a sentence (again, assuming that a blank is the delimiter). Thus in the sentence of Step 1, it would find "Smith:" and "Jones?", but not "Abrams". because "Abrams" is immediately followed by a carriage return. The punctuation marks are included in the names found.

Step 3 finds all the last names in a sentence (assuming that any nonletter is a delimiter). Thus it would find "Smith", "Jones", and "Abrams".

Step 4 extends Step 3 to a paragraph. In addition. when a sentence ends with "Mrs.", the program will print the first word in the next sentence.

Step 1

The pseudocode for Step I is

> *Read* Lead_word:
> *Read Sentence from the file:*
> *Find and print the word after* Lead_word

where, in our case, Lead_word is "Mrs.". This suggests the top-down diagram shown in Figure 11.7a. The pseudocode for procedure Finds is

> *Find the position of* Lead_word *in the sentence:*
> *Redefine the sentence so that the part from its beginning*
> *to the end of* Lead_word *is erased.*
> *Find the end of the first word in the redefined sentence:*
> *Copy that word to the printer.*

This is translated into procedure Finds. shown in Figure 11.7b(I), where the value of Position is the position of the beginning of Lead_word in the sentence and the value of Pos_next_word is the position of the beginning of the next word. To see how this works, let's examine the following: If, for instance, the original contents of Sentence are

H	e	l	l	o		M	r	s	.		S	m	i	t	h	;		a	n	d		M	r	s	.		J	o	n	e	s	?	
1	2	3	4	5	6	7	8	9	10	11	12	13	14	15	16	17	18	19	10	11	12	13	14	15	16	17	18	19	10	11	12	13	14

the value of Position is 7, the value of Pos_next_word is 12, and thus Copy(Sentence, Pos_next_word, To_end) becomes Copy(Sentence, 7, 300). We use 300 here to simplify the evaluation, since only the part of the string up to its end is copied. The redefined sentence, Rest, becomes

S	m	i	t	h	;		a	n	d		M	r	s	.		J	o	n	e	s	?
1	2	3	4	5	6	7	8	9	10	11	12	13	14	15	16	17	18	19	10	11	12

We implement *Find the end of the first word* be subtracting 1 from the position of the next blank, as shown in procedure End_word, Figure 11.7b(II). The value of this position, 6, is assigned to End_position. Thus Copy(Rest, 1, End_position) becomes Copy(Rest, 1, 6) and "Smith:" is assigned to Target_word.

Procedure Read_file has already been displayed in Figure 11.3a(I), but now it reads a different file, so we have saved it as READFIL1.PAS. The main program and the headings for the procedures are shown in Figure 11.7c and the running of the program in Figure 11.7d.

Step II

In order to find the word that follows each occurrence of Lead_word, let's rewrite procedure Finds. The pseudocode for the new version is

> *Find the position of* Lead_word *in the sentence;*
> WHILE *that position* <> 0 DO BEGIN
> > *Redefine the sentence so that the part from its beginning*
> > *to the end of* Lead_word *is erased.*
> > *Find the end of the first word in the redefined sentence;*
> > *Copy that word to the printer;*
> > *Find the position of* Lead_word *in the redefined sentence*

END {WHILE};

In order to search for each occurrence of Lead_word, change Rest := Copy(Sentence, Pos_next_word, To_end) in the previous version of procedure Finds to

Sentence:= Copy(Sentence, Pos_next_word, To_end);

as shown in Figure 11.8a. Redefining Sentence this way erases the sentence up to the word following Lead_word and allows the program in

Target_word:=Copy(Sentence, 1, End_position);

to search for a new last name each time the loop is executed. as shown in the table for Figure 11.8a. where End position indicates the end of the first word. If we save function End_word from the previous program as the Include file ENDWORD. we may include it in the present program. as shown in Figure 11.8b.

Step III

What's new here is that function End_word is rewritten so that when it finds the end of the first word in the redefined Sentence. it looks for any nonletter as the delimiter. Its pseudocode is

> *Set* Index *to 1:*
> WHILE *the current character is a letter* DO
>   *Increment* Index *by 1:*
>   *Since the last value of* Index *is for a nonletter.*
>   *subtract 1 from* Index

Because the boolean expression in the translation of the WHILE includes AND (Index <= Length(Sentence). as shown in Figure 11.9a. the function finds the last word in the sentence even if it is immediately followed by a CR/LF. We have included procedure Finds from the previous program as an Include file here. The results of running the program are shown in Figure 11.9b.

Step IV

Extends Step III to a program that reads a paragraph. In order to find a last name (Target_word) even if "Mrs." is the last word in the preceding sentence. do the following:

1. Alter procedure Finds so that it tests whether Lead_word is the last word in the sentence: this means that Target_word will be the first word in the next sentence. If it is. set the boolean VAR parameter. Next_sentence. to true in this procedure. as shown in Figure 11.10a(I):

    ```
    IF Pos_next_word >= length(Sentence) THEN
        Next_sentence:= True;
    ```

2. Add procedure First_word. which prints the first word in the sentence: see Figure 11.10a(II). This will be activated if the value of Next_sentence is True.

3. Add procedure Read_Parag. Figure 11.10a(III). so that you can see the paragraph before you make any alterations.

4. Add procedure Read_file. Figure 11.10a(IV). which reads each line of the paragraph. If the previous line ends with Lead_word. this procedure will direct the computer to print the first word in the next line.

The top-down diagram for the program is

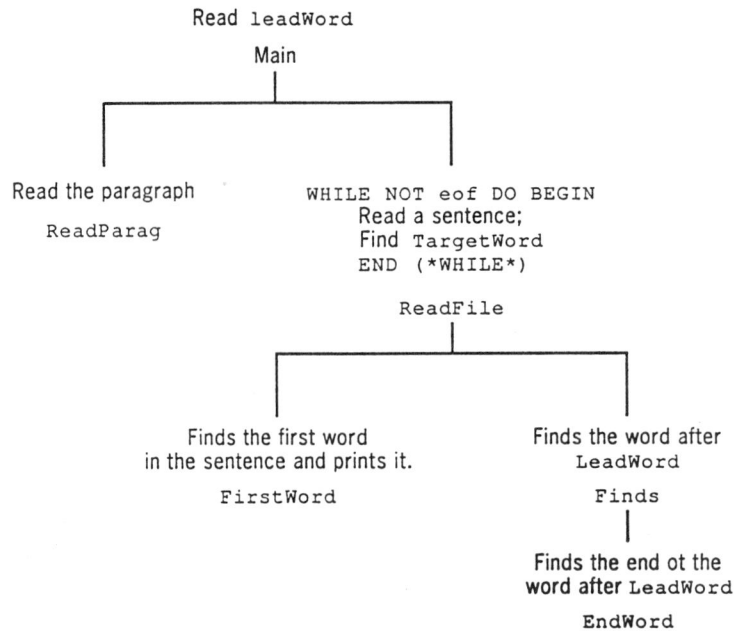

```
                        Read leadWord
                            Main
                             |
          +------------------+------------------+
          |                                     |
  Read the paragraph              WHILE NOT eof DO BEGIN
                                    Read a sentence;
     ReadParag                      Find TargetWord
                                  END (*WHILE*)

                                      ReadFile
                                         |
                    +--------------------+--------------------+
                    |                                         |
           Finds the first word                    Finds the word after
        in the sentence and prints it.                  LeadWord

              FirstWord                                    Finds
                                                             |
                                                  Finds the end ot the
                                                  word after LeadWord

                                                        EndWord
```

Figure 11.10*b* displays the main program, the include file references, and the headings for the procedures used that are not include files. Finally, the program is run in Figure 11.10*c*. The output displays the line number and the last names occurring on the line with that number. If you arrange this information in alphabetic order, you can construct an index.

TEST YOURSELF

QUESTION: The statement part of procedure Read_file is

```
BEGIN
   reset(Sentence_file);
   Next_sentence:= False;
   N:=0;
   WHILE NOT eof(Sentence_file) DO BEGIN
     N:= N + 1;
     readln(Sentence_file, Sentence);
     writeln('Sentence #', N, ':', Sentence);
     writeln('The words following ', Lead_word, ' are:');
     IF Next_sentence THEN BEGIN
       First_word(Sentence);
       Next_sentence:= False
     END {IF};
     Finds(Lead_Word, Sentence, Next_sentence)
   END {WHILE NOT eof};
   close(Sentence_file)
END {Read_file};
```

a. What happens if you exclude the Next_sentence: = False that precedes the IF?

b. What happens if you exclude the Next_sentence: = False that follows the IF?

c. What happens if you place the IF after the activation of Finds instead of before it?

ANSWER:

a. Since Next_sentence may be true, the program will print the first word on the first line.

b. When Next_sentence is true, not only will the first word of the next sentence be printed, but also the first word of the sentence after that sentence.

c. Since the first sentence ends with "Mrs.", the value of Next_sentence will be true. Because the IF follows, the program will print the first word of the first sentence instead of the first word of the second sentence.

FORMING AN INDEX
STEP I: FINDS THE WORD AFTER A GIVEN WORD

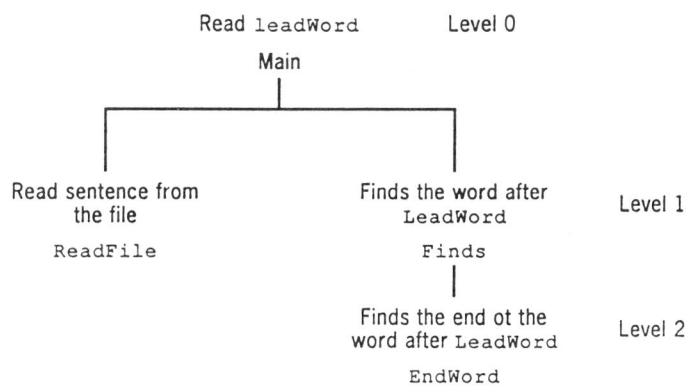

FIGURE 11.7a. The top-down diagram for a program that finds a word in a sentence following another word (called Lead_word) that is read into the program.

```
CONST Blank = ' ';
   To_end = 300;
TYPE Line = string[80];
PROCEDURE Finds(Lead_word :Line; VAR Sentence:Line);
{Finds the word after Lead_word}
VAR Rest, Target_word:Line;
   Pos_next_word, Word_length:word;
BEGIN
   Position:= Pos(Lead_word, Sentence);
   Word_length:= length(Lead_word) + 1;
   {...Eliminate Lead_word from sentence}
   Pos_next_word:= Position + Word_length;
   Rest:= Copy(Sentence, Pos_next_word, To_end);
   writeln('The rest of the sentence is :');
   writeln(Rest);
   {...Find the end of the next word}
   End_position:= End_word(Sentence);
   Target_word:=Copy(Rest, 1, End_position);
   writeln('The next word is ', Target_word);
END; {Finds}
```

FIGURE 11.7b(I). Finds the word after Lead_word by copying the part of the sentence following Lead_word to Rest and then printing the first word in Rest.

```
FUNCTION End_word(Sentence:Line):word;
{Finds the end of the next word in a sentence}
BEGIN
   End_word:= Pos(Blank, Sentence) − 1
END {END_WORD};
```

FIGURE 11.7b(II).   Finds the end of the first word in a sentence.

```
PROGRAM Replacement;
{Finds the word after the inputted word}
Uses CRT;
CONST Blank = ' ';
   To_end = 300;
TYPE Line = string[80];
VAR Lead_word, Sentence:Line;
   End_position, Position:word;
   Sentence_file:text;
FUNCTION End_word(Sentence:Line):word;
PROCEDURE Finds(Lead_word :Line; VAR Sentence:Line);
{$I Readfill}
BEGIN
   ClrScr;
   Read_file(Sentence);
   writeln('The sentence read was:');
   writeln(Sentence);
   writeln('Type the word preceding the desired word');
   readln(Lead_word);
   Finds(Lead_word, Sentence);
END.
```

FIGURE 11.7c.   Shows the main program, the activation of the Include file that reads the sentence, and the headings of the procedures used.

```
The sentence read was:
Hello Mrs. Smith; and Mrs. Jones? Do you know Mrs. Abrams
Type the word preceding the desired word
Mrs.
The rest of the sentence is :
Smith; and Mrs. Jones? Do you know Mrs. Abrams
The next word is Smith;
```

FIGURE 11.7d.   Running the program of Figure 11.7c.

```
PROGRAM Replacement;
{Extracts all occurrences of words that follows a target
substring in a string. The words must be terminated by blanks.}
Uses CRT;

CONST Blank = ' ';
   To_end = 300;
TYPE Line = string[80];
VAR Target_word, Lead_word, Sentence:Line;
   Sentence_file:text;

{$I ReadFill}
{$I Endword}

PROCEDURE Finds(Lead_word, Sentence:Line);
{Finds all the words that follow a substring}
VAR End_position, Pos_next_word, Word_length, Position:word;
   Target_word:Line;
BEGIN
   Word_length:= length(Lead_word) + 1;
   Position:= Pos(Lead_word, Sentence);
   writeln('The words to the right of each ', Lead_word, '
are:');
   WHILE Position <> 0 DO BEGIN
      {...Eliminate Lead_word from sentence}
      Pos_next_word:= Position + Word_length;
      Sentence:= Copy(Sentence, Pos_next_word, To_end);
      {...Find the ending of the next word}
      End_position:= End_word(Sentence);
      Target_word:=Copy(Sentence, 1, End_position);
      writeln(Target_word);
      {...Find next position of Lead_word}
      Position:= Pos(Lead_word, Sentence)
      END {WHILE}
   END; {Finds}
   BEGIN
      ClrScr;
      Read_file(Sentence);
      writeln('The sentence read was:');
      writeln(Sentence);
      writeln('Type the word preceding the desired word');
      readln(Lead_word);
      Finds(Lead_Word, Sentence);
   END.
```

FIGURE 11.8a.   Finds the word (including the possible punctuation following it) that follows each occurrence of Lead_word in the sentence by continually redefining the sentence as beginning after the last occurrence of Lead_word found.

Sentence on left-hand side of copy	Target_word
Smith; and Mrs. Jones? Do you know Mrs. Abrams	Smith;
Jones? Do you know Mrs. Abrams	Jones?
Abrams	Abrams

TABLE FOR FIGURE 11.8a. Each time `Sentence := Copy(Sentence, Pos_next_word, To_end)` is executed, the value of `Sentence` is changed, and so is that of `Target_word`.

```
The sentence read was:
Hello Mrs. Smith; and Mrs. Jones? Do you know Mrs. Abrams
Type the word preceding the desired word
Mrs.
The words to the right of each Mrs. are:
Smith;
Jones?
```

FIGURE 11.8b. Running the program of Figure 11.8a. The program doesn't find "Abrams", since it is terminated by a carriage return. We correct for this in the next program.

FORMING AN INDEX
STEP III: FINDS THE WORD AFTER EACH OCCURRENCE OF A GIVEN WORD EVEN IF THE WORD ENDS WITH A CARRIAGE RETURN

```
PROGRAM Replacement;
{Extracts all occurrences of words that follow a target
substring in a string. The words are terminated by any
punctuation or end-of line mark}

Uses CRT;
CONST Blank = ' ';
   To_end = 300;
TYPE Line = string[80];
VAR Target_word, Lead_word, Sentence:Line;
   Sentence_file:text;

FUNCTION End_word(Sentence:Line):word;
{Finds the end of the next word in a sentence}
VAR Index:integer;
BEGIN
  Index:= 1;
  WHILE (Sentence[Index] IN ['a'..'z', 'A'..'Z'])
    AND (Index <= Length(Sentence) ) DO
      Index:= Index + 1;
  End_word:= Index - 1
END {END_WORD};

{$I ReadFill}
{$I Finds}

BEGIN
  ClrScr;
  Read_file(Sentence);
```

```
        writeln('The sentence read was:');
        writeln(Sentence);
        writeln('Type the word preceding the desired word');
        readln(Lead_word);
        Finds(Lead_Word, Sentence);
        close(Sentence_file)
   END.
```

FIGURE 11.9a.   Finds the word (excluding possible punctuation) that follows each occurrence of Lead_word in the sentence by continually redefining the sentence as beginning after the last occurrence of Lead_word found. To detect a word terminated by a carriage return and not by punctuation, we include an additional test.

```
   The sentence read was:
   Hello Mrs. Smith; and Mrs. Jones? Do you know Mrs. Abrams
   Type the word preceding the desired word
   Mrs.
   The words to the right of each Mrs. are:
   Smith
   Jones
   Abrams
```

FIGURE 11.9b.   Running the program of Figure 11.9a.

FORMING AN INDEX
STEP IV: FINDS THE WORD AFTER EACH OCCURRENCE OF A GIVEN WORD EVEN IF THE WORD ENDS WITH A CARRIAGE RETURN OR OCCURS AS THE FIRST WORD IN THE NEXT SENTENCE

```
   PROCEDURE Finds(Lead_word, Sentence:String_type;
   VAR Next_sentence:boolean);
   {...Finds all the words that follow a substring}
   VAR End_position, Pos_next_word, Word_length, Position:word;
     Targetword:String_type;
   BEGIN
     Word_length:= length(Lead_word) + 1;
     Position:= Pos(Lead_word, Sentence);
     WHILE Position <> 0 DO BEGIN
       {...Eliminate Lead_word from sentence}
       Pos_next_word:= Position + Word_length;
       IF Pos_next_word >= length(Sentence) THEN
         Next_sentence:= True;
       Sentence:= Copy(Sentence, Pos_next_word, To_end);
       {...Find the ending of the next word}
       End_position:= End_word(Sentence);
       Target_word:=Copy(Sentence, 1, End_position);
       writeln(Target_word);
```

```
        Position:= Pos(Lead_word, Sentence)
    END {WHILE}
  END; {Finds}
```

FIGURE 11.10a(I). The procedure of Figure 11.8a rewritten so that it detects if the word following the substring occurs on the next line.

```
PROCEDURE First_word(Sentence:String_type);
{...If the previous Lead_word was at the end of the last sentence,
... this finds the first word}
VAR End_position:word;
  Target_word:String_type;
BEGIN
  End_position:= End_word(Sentence);
  Target_word:=Copy(Sentence, 1, End_position);
  writeln(Target_word)
END {First_word};
```

FIGURE 11.10a(II). If the previous Lead_word was at the end of the last sentence, this procedure finds the first word in the current sentence.

```
        PROCEDURE Read_Paragraph(VAR Sentence_file:text);
        {Reads a paragraph from a file}
        VAR Sentence:String_type;
        BEGIN
          assign(Sentence_file, 'Parag.dat');
          reset(Sentence_file);
          writeln('The paragraph read was:');
          writeln;
          WHILE NOT eof(Sentence_file) DO BEGIN
            readln(Sentence_file, Sentence);
            writeln(Sentence);
          END{WHILE NOT eof};
          writeln
        END {Read};
```

FIGURE 11.10a(III). Reads a paragraph from a file.

```
PROCEDURE Read_file(VAR Sentence_file:text; Lead_word:String_type);
{Finds target words}
VAR Next_sentence:boolean;
  N:integer;
  Sentence:String_type;
BEGIN
  reset(Sentence_file);
  Next_sentence:= False;
  N:=0;
  WHILE NOT eof(Sentence_file) DO BEGIN
    N:= N + 1;
    readln(Sentence_file, Sentence);
    writeln('Sentence #', N, ':', Sentence);
    writeln('The words following ', Lead_word, ' are:');
    IF Next_sentence THEN BEGIN
      First_word(Sentence);
      Next_sentence:= False
    END {IF};
    Finds(Lead_Word, Sentence, Next_sentence)
  END {WHILE NOT eof};
  close(Sentence_file)
END {Read_file};
```

FIGURE 11.10a(IV).   Finds all the target words in the paragraph.

```
PROGRAM Search;
{...Prints all occurrences of words in a file that follows
...a target substring in a string. The words are terminated
...by any punctuation or end-of line mark. The file consists
...of a paragraph}
Uses CRT;
CONST Blank = ' ';
   TO_end = 300;
TYPE String_type = string[80];
VAR Target_word, Lead_word :String_type;
   Sentence_file:text;

{$I Endword}

PROCEDURE First_word(Sentence:String_type);
PROCEDURE Finds(Lead_word, Sentence:String_type;
        VAR Next_sentence:boolean);

PROCEDURE Read_Paragraph(VAR Sentence_file:text);

PROCEDURE Read_file(VAR Sentence_file:text; Lead_word:String_type);

BEGIN
  ClrScr;
  Read_Paragraph(Sentence_file);
  writeln('Type the word preceding the desired word');
  readln(Lead_word);
  Read_file(Sentence_file, Lead_word)
END.
```

FIGURE 11.10b.   The main program and the headings of the procedures it uses.

```
The paragraph read was:
Hello Mrs. Smith, Mrs. Jones, and Mrs.
Abrams. Lend me your ears. How are
Mrs. Davis; and Mrs. Cook?

Type the word preceding the desired word
Mrs.
Sentence #1:Hello Mrs. Smith, Mrs. Jones, and Mrs.
The words following Mrs. are:
Smith
Jones

Sentence #2:Abrams. Lend me your ears. How are
The words following Mrs. are:
Abrams
Senence #3:Mrs. Davis; and Mrs. Cook?
The words following Mrs. are:
Davis
Cook
```

FIGURE 11.10c.   Running the program of Figure 11.10a.

14.6

LONG INTEGER ADDITION—FIXED LENGTH

MOTIVATION

All compilers are limited in the number of digits they can accommodate in an integer value—we know that the value of the maximum integer is maxint. There is also a maximum number of digits that the compiler can accommodate in a real value—let's say it's 8 digits on the Pascal compiler we are using. When we square 54321.0 on a hand calculator we get the ten-digit result: 2950771041; however when we do the calculation on our Pascal compiler, we get a number that is accurate to only 8 digits, 2950771034. The two right-most digits, 3 and 4, are not accurate. **
We now demonstrate a method that will enable us to obtain as many digits of accuracy as we want.

**See, for instance, *FORTRAN 77*, by S. Marateck, Academic Press, New York (1983), p. 558.

We begin by defining a long integer as one that can have a value greater than the value of maxint. We are able to represent a long integer by storing each of its digits in a different element of an array. In order to add long integers we must instruct the computer to add the integers in the same way we add them by hand: For instance, to add 567 and 689 we add the first digits (counting from the right, i.e., 7 + 9) of the two integers, carry the tens digit (here, 1) and add that to the sum of the second digits (6 + 8) of the two integers. We repeat this process until all the corresponding digits are added.

Looking at this process in detail, we get

```
  11
 567
+ 689
1256
```

When we add 7 and 9 we get the intermediate sum 16. We record the units digit, 6, and carry the tens digit, 1. We then add this 1 to the sum of the 6 and 8 and we get 15. We record the units digit, 5, and carry the tens digit, 1. We continue this process until all the digits are added.

We know that the value of the units digit can vary from 0 to 9. The value of the tens digit can be either 0 or 1 for the following reason. When we add the digits with the maximum value, 9 + 9, the intermediate sum is 18 and we carry the 1. If the next two digits are again 9s, the intermediate sum is 9 + 9 + the carry of 1. We then get the result 19, which is the maximum intermediate sum obtainable. The value of the carry can never exceed 1. We will use this information to declare as a subrange the variable representing the tens digit in Carry:0..1, the variable representing the units digit in Units:0..9;, and the variable representing the intermediate sum in Total:0..19;.

PROGRAM DESIGN

We wish to write a program that adds two integers of different lengths, for example, 1234 and 654321. In order to simplify writing this program, we write it in two stages. The first adds two integers of the same length. Once we have written this, it is easier to write a program that adds two integers of different lengths.

In order to read integers greater than maxint, we must read each individual digit as a character. We then store each digit in an element of an array. The first program we consider adds two integers, each of which contains the same number of digits, here six.

The procedure for Convert is straightforward and is shown in Figure 14.8a(I).

We store the digits of an integer in the array as you would expect, that is, we place the highest order digit in the first element of the array, the next to highest order digit in the second element, and so on. The integers 432178 and 987654 are stored as

```
Num1       | 4 | 3 | 2 | 1 | 7 | 8 |
Subscript    1   2   3   4   5   6

Num2       | 9 | 8 | 7 | 6 | 5 | 4 |
Subscript    1   2   3   4   5   6
```

We sum the two integers by first adding the sixth elements of each array, then the fifth elements, and so on. The pseudocode is:

Set Carry to zero;
FOR *the 6th to 1st element of the arrays* DO BEGIN
    Add corresponding elements plus Carry;
    Separate the intermediate sum into units and tens digits;
    Place units digit in Final array;
    Set Carry to tens digit
END *;*
Store the last carry in zeroth element of Final

This translates in procedure Sum into

```
Carry:= 0;
FOR K:= Nmax DOWNTO 1 DO BEGIN
    Total:= (Num1[K] + Num2[K]) + Carry;
    Units:= Total MOD 10;
    Carry:= Total DIV 10;
    Final [K]:= Units;
    write( Final [K]:1)
END (* FOR K *);
```

as is shown in Figure 14.8a(II). When we print the sum in procedure Print we must include the result of the final carry—it's stored in Final[0]—so we use 0 as the initial value of the loop control variable and write FOR K:= 0 TO Nmax DO write(Final[K]:1), as is shown in Figure 14.8a(III). The entire program is presented in Figure 14.8b and the results of running the program appear in Figure 14.8c.

ADDING TWO LONG INTEGERS THAT ARE BOTH LARGER THAN MAXINT—STEP I: EACH INTEGER HAS THE SAME NUMBER OF DIGITS

```
CONST Nmax = 6;

TYPE  Digs = 0..9;
      IntArray = ARRAY[1..Nmax] OF digs;
      DigArray = ARRAY[0..Nmax ] OF digs;

PROCEDURE Convert(VAR Digit: IntArray);
(* Stores the digits in the Number in the array "Digit" *)
VAR J, K: integer;
    ch: '0'..'9';
BEGIN
    K:= 0;
    writeln('Type your ', Nmax, '-Digit Number');
    FOR J:= 1 TO Nmax DO BEGIN
        read(ch);
        K:= K + 1;
        Digit[K]:= ord(ch) - ord('0')
    END (* FOR *);
    writeln('The Number read was');
    FOR K:= 1 TO Nmax DO
        write( Digit[K]:1);
    writeln;
    readln
END(* Convert *);
```

FIGURE 14.8a(I).

Converts each digit read as a character into an integer value and stores the value in an element of the array Digit.

```
PROCEDURE Sum(VAR Final: DigArray; Num1, Num2: IntArray);
VAR K: integer;
    Carry:0..1;
    Units:0..9;
    Total: 0..19;
BEGIN
    Carry:= 0;
    writeln('Summing from the low to high digits, w/low
            on left, we get');
    FOR K:= Nmax DOWNTO 1 DO BEGIN
        Total:= (Num1[K] + Num2[K]) + Carry;
        Units:= Total MOD 10;
        Carry:= Total DIV 10;
        Final [K]:= Units;
        write( Final [K]:1)
    END (* FOR K *);
    Final [0]:= Carry;
    writeln( Final [0]:1)
END (* Sum *);
```

FIGURE 14.8a(II). Forms the sum of corresponding elements of Num1 and Num2, records the low-order (units) digit in an element of Final and carries the high-order (tens) digit for the next sum.

```
PROCEDURE Print(Final: DigArray; Nmax: integer);
VAR K:integer;
BEGIN
     write('Sum=');
     FOR K:= 0 TO Nmax DO
          write( Final[K]:1)
END (* Print *);
```

FIGURE 14.8a(III). Prints the sum.

```
PROGRAM Addition2(input, output);
CONST Nmax = 6;
TYPE IntArray = ARRAY[1..Nmax] OF integer;
     DigArray = ARRAY[0..Nmax ] OF integer;
VAR Num1, Num2: IntArray;
    Final:DigArray;

PROCEDURE Convert(VAR Digit: IntArray);

PROCEDURE Sum(VAR Final: DigArray; Num1, Num2: IntArray);

PROCEDURE Print(Final: DigArray; Nmax: integer);

BEGIN (* Addition2 *)
     Convert(Num1);
     Convert(Num2);
     Sum(Final, Num1, Num2);
     print(Final, Nmax)
END.
```

FIGURE 14.8b. The main program and the headings for the procedures used.

```
Type your 6-Digit Number
432156
The Number read was
432156
Type your 6-Digit Number
987654
The Number read was
987654
Summing from the low to high digits, w/low on left, we get
0189141
Sum=1419810
```

FIGURE 14.8c. Running the program of Figure 14.8b.

14.7

LONG INTEGER ADDITION—VARIABLE LENGTH

We now write a program that adds two integers of any lengths. In procedure ReadDigits, shown in Figure 14.9a(I), we read the digits of an integer into an array, and at the same time determine how many digits are in the integer. Let's say that the first and second integers read are 7888 and 567999, respectively. The array Num1 will contain 7888 and Num2 will contain 567999. The arrays will appear as follows:

Num1	|7|8|8|8|	Num2	|5|6|7|9|9|9|
Subscript	1 2 3 4	Subscript	1 2 3 4 5 6

In order to add these two integers as we did in the previous program, we must first determine which one has more digits. We then align the two integers, so that lowest order digits in both integers (the 8 in the first integer and the 9 in the second one, in our example) are in the same column.

```
    7888
+ 567999
  575887
```

In order to do this with the elements of the arrays in our example, we must shift each of the digits in Num1 two elements, obtaining

Num1	|0|0|7|8|8|8|	Num2	|5|6|7|9|9|9|
Subscript	1 2 3 4 5 6	Subscript	1 2 3 4 5 6

Note that we have placed zeros in the first two elements of Num1 so that we can add the contents of these elements to the corresponding elements of Num2. Now the addition can proceed. In the pseudocode that describes the shifting, *Big* is the number of digits in the larger integer, and *Small* is the number of digits in the smaller one. The shifting is done on array *Number* that stores the smaller of the two integers.

Set Diff equal to Big minus Small;
Set the first Diff elements of a temporary array to zero;
Copy the elements of Number into the remaining elements of the temporary array;
Copy the temporary array back into Number.

This translates into procedure Shift, shown in Figure 14.9a(II). The procedure for Sum, shown in Figure 14.9a(III), is almost identical to the one used in the previous program. The pseudocode for the main program is

Read the digits of the first integer into array Num1;
Read the digits of the second integer into array Num2;
IF *first integer is longer then the second* THEN BEGIN
    Shift the second integer;
    Set MaxLen to length of first integer
  END (* IF first *)
ELSE IF *second integer is longer than the first* THEN BEGIN
    Shift the first integer;
    Set MaxLen to length of second integer
  END (* IF second *)
  ELSE (* second and first integers have the same length *)
    Set MaxLen to length of first (or second) integer;
Sum the corresponding first MaxLen digits of the arrays.
Print the results.

where *Shift* is the pseudocode we just discussed. We use two procedures to print the long integers. The first one, `Print`, is shown in Figure 14.9*a*(IV). It prints the value of the larger of the long integers—it consists of FOR K:= 1 TO Big DO write(Final[K]).

The second one, `FinalPrint`, is shown in Figure 14.9*a*(V). It prints the sum of the two integers. The sum of the two integers is stored in the array `Final`. If the sum of the two high-order digits produces a carry, a 1 is stored `Final[0]`, otherwise a 0 is stored there. For instance, if we add 611111 and 711111 the sum of the 6 and the 7 produces a carry of 1. This 1 is stored in `Final[0]`. On the other hand, if a 0 is stored in `Final[0]`, procedure `FinalPrint` does not print this zero.

The main program is shown in Figure 14.9*b* and the results of running the program are shown in Figure 14.9*c*.

ADDING TWO LONG INTEGERS THAT ARE BOTH LARGER THAN MAXINT—STEP II: THE INTEGERS ARE NOT THE SAME LENGTH

```
CONST MaxSubsc = 10;
Type SubscRange = 0..MaxSubsc;
     Digs = 0..9;
     DigitArray = ARRAY[SubscRange] OF Digs;

PROCEDURE ReadDigits (VAR NumDigits:SubscRange; VAR
                       Digit:DigitArray);
(* Determines how many Digits in number and reads into an array *)
VAR ch: '0'..'9';
BEGIN
     NumDigits:= 0;
     writeln('Type your  number with Digits only');
     WHILE NOT eoln DO begin
          read(ch);
          NumDigits:= NumDigits + 1;
          Digit[NumDigits]:= ord(ch) - ord('0')
     END (* WHILE *);
     readln (* otherwise computer will read past the eoln mark *)
end (* ReadDigits *);
```

FIGURE 14.9*a*(I).   Converts each digit read as a character into an integer value and stores the value in an element of the array `Digit`.   Also counts the number of digits in the integer.

```
PROCEDURE Shift(VAR Number: DigitArray; Big, Small:
                SubscRange);
(* shifts the smaller number so that it aligns with the
 larger one *)
VAR Temp: DigitArray;
    L, Diff, K: SubscRange;
BEGIN
     Diff:= Big - Small;
     FOR K:= 1 TO Diff DO
         Temp[K]:= 0;
     L:= 0;
     FOR K:= Diff + 1 TO Big DO BEGIN
         L:= L + 1;
         Temp[K]:= Number[L]
     END(*  FOR-K *);
     writeln('Larger length = ', Big, ', Smaller length
             = ', Small);
     Number:= Temp (* Store shifted number back in "Number" *);
     FOR K:= 1 TO Big DO write( Number[K]:1);
     writeln(' is the shifted ', Small:2, ' digit number.');
END(* Shift *);
```

FIGURE 14.9a(II). Aligns the smaller of the two integers so that when it is added to the larger the one, the correct digits will be added.

```
PROCEDURE Sum(VAR Final:DigitArray; Num1, Num2:DigitArray;
              MaxLen:SubscRange);
(* Sums the two numbers *)
VAR Carry:0..1;
    Units:0..9;
    Total:0..19;
    K: SubscRange;
BEGIN
     Carry:= 0;
     FOR K:= MaxLen DOWNTO 1 DO BEGIN
         Total:= (Num1[K] + Num2[K]) + Carry;
         Units:= Total MOD 10;
         Carry:= Total DIV 10;
         Final [K]:= Units;
     END (* FOR K *);
     Final[0]:= Carry
END (* Sum *);
```

FIGURE 14.9a(III). Forms the sum of corresponding elements of Num1 and Num2, records the low-order (units) digit in an element of Final and carries the high-order (tens) digit for the next sum. This differs from the Sum in the last program since now the number of digits, MaxLen, in the integer is passed to the procedure.

```
PROCEDURE Print(Final: DigitArray; Big: SubscRange);
(* Prints the larger of the two numbers to be added *)
VAR K:SubscRange;
begin
     FOR K:= 1 TO Big DO
          write( Final[K]:1);
     writeln(' is the ', Big:2, ' digit number.');
end (* Print *);
```

FIGURE 14.9a(IV). Prints the larger of the two integers to be added. The smaller one is printed in Shift.

```
PROCEDURE FinalPrint(Final:DigitArray; MaxLen:SubscRange);
(* Prints sum of two numbers, without printing a possible
 leading zero *)
VAR K :SubscRange;
    Min:0..1;
BEGIN
     writeln('---------------');
     IF Final[0] = 0 THEN Min :=1 ELSE Min:= 0;
     (* Final[0] means the sum of last two digits did not
      produce a carry *)
     FOR K:=  Min  TO MaxLen DO
         write( Final [K]:1);
     writeln(' is the sum.')
END (* FinalPrint *);
```

FIGURE 14.9a(V). Prints the sum of the two integers but does not print any leading zeros.

```
PROGRAM Addition3(input, output);
CONST MaxSubsc = 10;
Type SubscRange = 0..MaxSubsc;
     Digs = 0..9;
     DigitArray = ARRAY[SubscRange] OF Digs;
VAR Final, Num1, Num2: DigitArray;
    Len1, Len2, MaxLen: SubscRange;

PROCEDURE ReadDigits (VAR NumDigits:SubscRange; VAR
                      Digit:DigitArray);

PROCEDURE Shift(VAR Number: DigitArray; Big, Small:
                SubscRange);

PROCEDURE Sum(VAR Final:DigitArray; Num1, Num2:DigitArray;
              MaxLen:SubscRange);

PROCEDURE Print(Final: DigitArray; Big: SubscRange);

PROCEDURE FinalPrint(Final:DigitArray; MaxLen:SubscRange);

BEGIN (* Addition3 *)
     ReadDigits( Len1, Num1);
     ReadDigits( Len2, Num2);
     (* Determine which integer is shorter and shift it
      so that you can add the two integers from the low to
      the high digits *)
     IF Len1 > Len2 THEN BEGIN
             Shift(Num2, Len1, Len2);
             Print(Num1, Len1);
             MaxLen:= Len1
        END
     ELSE IF Len2 > Len1 THEN BEGIN
          Shift(Num1, Len2, Len1);
          Print(Num2, Len2);
          MaxLen:= Len2
     END
     ELSE
        MaxLen:= Len1; (* They are equal *)
     Sum( Final, Num1, Num2, MaxLen);
     FinalPrint(Final, MaxLen)
END.
```

FIGURE 14.9b. The main program and the headings for the procedures used.

```
Type your  number with Digits only
7888
Type your  number with Digits only
567999
Larger length = 6, Smaller length = 4
007888 is the shifted  4 digit number.
567999 is the  6 digit number.
----------------
575887 is the sum.
```

FIGURE 14.9c. Running the program of Figure 14.9b.

14.8

MULTIPLYING A LONG INTEGER BY A TWO-DIGIT INTEGER

The rest of the chapter is devoted to writing a program that uses long integers to calculate factorials. We know that N!= N * (N–1)!. We will write a program that will calculate N! where N is an integer smaller than maxint—we'll call it a regular integer—and (N–1)! is a long integer. For instance 15! is the product of 15 and 14!, that is, the regular integer 15 and the long integer 14!, that is, 87178291200.

As we normally do, we simplify the problem by resolving it into several relatively simple steps.

Our first step is to present an algorithm for multiplying a long integer by a regular integer. It is an extension of the method for multiplying integers we learned in grade school. Let's say that we want to multiply 1234 (a long integer) by 26 (a regular integer.) We will proceed by multiplying each of the digits in 1234 by 26.

1. Multiply 26 by 4. We obtain 104—record the 4 as the lowest order digit of the product and carry the 10 (the leading digits). The product so far is 4.

2. Multiply 26 by 3. We obtain 78; add to this the previous carry of 10 and obtain 88—record the 8 as the next digit in the product, and carry the 8. The product so far is 84.

3. Multiply 26 by 2. We obtain 52; add to this the previous carry of 8 and obtain 60—record the 0 as the next digit in the product, and carry the 6. The product so far is 084.

4. Multiply 26 by 1. We obtain 26; add to this the previous carry of 6 and obtain 32—record the 2 and carry the 3. Since we are now finished, we record the 3 as well. The final value of the product is 32084.

We will store the long integer in *Top* and the regular one in *Bottom*. The pseudocode for our long integer multiplication is

> *Set Carry to zero;*
> FOR *the 6th to 1st element of the arrays* DO BEGIN
>   *Multiply Bottom by the indicated element of Top;*
>   *Add Carry to this product;*
>   *Separate product into units and leading digits;*
>   *Place units digit in the indicated element of array Product;*
>   *Set Carry to leading digits*
> END ;
> *Store the last carry in zeroth element of Product*

An example of how we separate the intermediate product into units and digits is the following: When we multiply 26 by 4 obtaining 104, we get the units digit 4 from 104 MOD 10 and the leading digit 10 from 104 DIV 10. The pseudocode therefore translates into

```
PROCEDURE Multiply(Top:IntArr; Bottom, LengthTop:integer;
                   VAR Product:IntArr);
(* Long integer multiplication. Bottom is the 2-digit
  integer *)
VAR  Carry,Digit, Num, T:integer;
BEGIN
     Carry:= 0;
     (* Multiply from low order to high order digits *)
     FOR T:= LengthTop DOWNTO 1 DO BEGIN
         Num:= Bottom * Top[T] + Carry;
         Digit:= Num MOD 10;
         Carry:= Num DIV 10;
         Product[T]:= digit
     END (* FOR T *);
     Product[0]:= Carry;
END; (* Multiply *)
```

where LengthTop is the number of digits in Top (Figure 14.10a).

A program written to test a subprogram is called a *driver program*. We have written the main program shown in Figure 14.10b as a driver for procedure Multiply. Therefore we have opted to generate the data in the program itself. The results of running the program are shown in Figure 14.10b.

MULTIPLYING A LONG INTEGER BY A STANDARD ONE

```
CONST MaxSubsc = 10;
TYPE IntArr = ARRAY[0..MaxSubsc] of integer;

PROCEDURE Multiply(Top:IntArr; Bottom, LengthTop:integer;
                   VAR Product:IntArr);
(* Long integer multiplication. Bottom is the 2-digit
 integer *)
VAR  Carry,Digit, Num, T:integer;
BEGIN
     Carry:= 0;
     (* Multiply from low order to high order digits *)
     FOR T:= LengthTop DOWNTO 1 DO BEGIN
         Num:= Bottom * Top[T] + Carry;
         Digit:= Num MOD 10;
         Carry:= Num DIV 10;
         Product[T]:= digit
     END (* FOR T *);
     Product[0]:= Carry;
END; (* Multiply *)
```

FIGURE 14.10a. Follows same technique we learned in grade school for multiplication except that now the number carried is larger than 9. If Bottom is 78 and Top[1] is 6, the product is 468. The 8 is stored in Product and the 46 is carried.

```
PROGRAM Test(input, output);
(* Multiplies a Long integer by a 2-digit one *)
CONST MaxSubsc = 10;
TYPE IntArr = ARRAY[0..MaxSubsc] of integer;
VAR Top, Product: IntArr;
    T, Bottom, LengthTop: integer;

PROCEDURE Multiply(Top:IntArr; Bottom, LengthTop:integer;
                   VAR Product:IntArr);

BEGIN (* Test *)
     LengthTop:= 6;
     FOR T:= 1 to LengthTop DO
         Top[T]:= T;
     (* Thus Top is 123456 *)
     Bottom:= 78;
     Multiply( Top, Bottom, LengthTop, Product);
     write('78 * 123456 = ');
     FOR T:= 0 TO LengthTop DO
         write( Product[T]:1)
END.
```

FIGURE 14.10b. The main program and the heading for the procedure used.

```
78 * 123456 = 9629568
```

FIGURE 14.10c. Running the program of Figure 14.10b.

14.9

USING LONG INTEGER MULTIPLICATION TO CALCULATE FACTORIALS

The next step is to write a program that produces a factorial such that all the digits are printed contiguously. For example, 14! would be printed as 87178291200.

The pseudocode for calculating N!, where *Top* and *Product* are long integers, and *Bottom* is a regular integer is:

Set Top to 1;
FOR *Bottom* := 1 TO N DO BEGIN
    Calculate Product by long multiplication of Top by Bottom;
    Set Top to Product
END

In the previous program we knew how many digits were in the array Top—it was 6—and we multiplied each of them by Bottom. Therefore we did not have to worry about multiplying Bottom by an element of Top that was undefined. This is not the case in the factorial program because the number of digits in Top will increase as the value of Bottom increases. Consequently we can encounter the following difficulty: If we calculate 5! (which is 120), and Top originally contains, for instance, the random digits 654321, the 120 is stored in the three highest elements and the result is 654120. The three first digits (654) are wrong—they should be all zero!

To avoid the possibility of getting the wrong answer by multiplying an undefined element by Bottom, we zero all the elements of Top—the number of elements is given by the value of LengthTop—in procedure Zero shown in Figure 14.11a(I). We write FOR K:= 1 TO LengthTop DO Product[K]:= 0. Note that we have chosen the value of LengthTop to be 80 so that we can calculate large factorials.

Setting the elements of Top to zero ultimately causes difficulties as we now explain: If we set the value of LengthTop to 6 and calculate 5!, the final contents of Product would be

```
Product     |0|0|0|1|2|0|
           ─────────────────
Subscript    1 2 3 4 5 6
```

where the three zeros to the left of the 120 are called *leading zeros*. When we print the value of Product, the result contains leading zeros. The pseudocode to suppress these leading zeros when the value of Product is printed, is

Determine how many leading zeros Product contains;
Print the elements of Product that do not contain leading zeros.

We refine this to:

Set Count to 1;
WHILE *there are leading zeros* DO
    Increase Count by 1.
FOR *elements from Count* TO *LengthTop* DO
    Print the contents of the array

The procedure, Format, that does this is shown in Figure 14.11a(II).

To initialize Top to 1, we place the 1 in the highest numbered element of Top we will use, since this position corresponds to the lowest order digit. We thus write Top[LengthTop]:= 1.

The main program is shown in Figure 14.11b and the program is run in Figure 14.11c.

EVALUATING FACTORIALS USING LONG INTEGERS

```
CONST LengthTop = 80;

TYPE OneDim = ARRAY[0..LengthTop] OF integer;

PROCEDURE Zero(VAR Product: OneDim; LengthTop: integer);
(* Zeros an array *)
VAR K: integer;
BEGIN
     FOR K:= 1 TO LengthTop DO
         Product[K]:= 0
END (* Zero *);
```

FIGURE 14.11a(I). We must zero the elements of `Product`, otherwise we will get the wrong result.

```
PROCEDURE Format(Product: OneDim; Length: integer);
(* Formats output so there are no leading zeros *)
VAR K, Count:integer;
BEGIN
     Count:= 1;
      WHILE Product[Count] = 0 DO (* How many leading zeros? *)
          Count:= Count + 1;
     FOR K:= Count  TO Length DO
         write(Product[K]:1);
     writeln
END (* Format *);
```

FIGURE 14.11a(II). Suppresses leading zeros in the resulting long integer; they were stored there by procedure `Zero`.

```
Program Test(input, output);
(* Calculates factorials using long integer  *)
(* Formats the output so that there are no leading zeros *)
CONST LengthTop = 80;

TYPE OneDim = ARRAY[0..LengthTop] OF integer;
VAR Top, Product: OneDim;
    Nfact, T, Bottom: integer;

PROCEDURE Multiply(Top:OneDim; Bottom, LengthTop :integer;
                   VAR Product:OneDim);

PROCEDURE Format(Product: OneDim; Length: integer);

PROCEDURE Zero(VAR Product: OneDim; LengthTop: integer);

BEGIN (* Test *)
     Zero(Top, LengthTop);
     Top[LengthTop]:= 1;
     writeln('Type the number for which you want the
             factorial');
     readln(Nfact);
     FOR Bottom:= 1 TO Nfact DO BEGIN
         Multiply( Top, Bottom, LengthTop, Product);
         Top:= Product;
         write(Bottom, '!=');
         Format(Product, LengthTop)
     END (* FOR *);
END.
```

FIGURE 14.11b. The main program and the headings for the procedures used.

```
Type the number for which you want the factorial
10
1!=1
2!=2
3!=6
4!=24
5!=120
6!=720
7!=5040
8!=40320
9!=362880
10!=3628800
```

FIGURE 14.11c. Running the program of Figure 14.11b.

14.10

INSERTING BLANKS IN THE FACTORIAL TO MAKE RESULTS MORE READABLE

In order to make the results more readable we now show how to insert blanks in the answer in the places where we would normally put commas. An answer like 3628800 would be printed as 3 628 800. The pseudocode is:

Determine how many digits precede the first occurrence of a comma in Product and set it equal to Remainder.
Insert a blank to the right of these digits and in every fourth position until the end of Product.

We translate this into the altered version of procedure Format shown in Figure 14.12a, where the first line of the above pseudocode becomes

```
Remainder:= NumDigits MOD 3;
```

and where the value of NumDigits is the number of digits excluding the leading zeros in the answer. The main program is shown in Figure 14.12b and the results of running the program are shown in Figure 14.12c.

EVALUATING FACTORIALS USING LONG INTEGERS SO THAT THERE IS A BLANK WHERE A COMMA WOULD ORDINARILY BE

```
Program Test(input, output);
(* Calculates factorials using long integer  *)
(* Formats the output so that there are no leading zeros *)
(* Places blanks every 3 places *)
CONST LengthTop = 80;
TYPE IntArr = ARRAY[0..LengthTop] of integer;

PROCEDURE Format(Product: IntArr; Length: integer);
(* Formats output so there are no leading zeros and blanks
 every 3 places *)
CONST Blank = ' ';
VAR K, J, Remainder, NumDigits, Count:integer;
BEGIN
     Count:= 1;
     WHILE Product[Count] = 0 DO (* How many leading zeros? *)
          Count:= Count + 1;
     NumDigits:= Length - Count + 1;
     Remainder:= NumDigits MOD 3;
     J:= 0;
     FOR K:= Count  TO Length DO Begin
          J:= J + 1;
          (* Insert a blank every 3 places from the right *)
          IF (((J - Remainder -1) MOD 3) = 0)   THEN
            write(Blank);
          write(Product[K]:1)
     END (* FOR *);
     writeln
END (* Format *);
```

FIGURE 14.12a. Inserts a blank in the factorial every three places from the right.

```
Program Test(input, output);
(* Calculates factorials using long integer  *)
(* Formats the output so that there are no leading zeros *)
(* Places blanks every 3 places *)
CONST LengthTop = 80;
TYPE IntArr = ARRAY[0..LengthTop] of integer;
VAR Top, Product: IntArr;
    Nfact, T, Bottom: integer;

PROCEDURE Multiply(Top:IntArr; Bottom, LengthTop :integer;
                   VAR Product:IntArr);

PROCEDURE Format(Product: IntArr; Length: integer);

PROCEDURE Zero(VAR Product: IntArr; LengthTop: integer);

BEGIN (* Test *)
      Zero(Top, LengthTop);
      Top[LengthTop]:= 1;
      writeln('Type the number for which you want the
              factorial');
      readln(Nfact);
      FOR Bottom:= 1 TO Nfact DO BEGIN
          Multiply( Top, Bottom, LengthTop, Product);
          Top:= Product;
          write(Bottom, '!=');
          Format(Product, LengthTop)
      END (* FOR *);
END.
```

FIGURE 14.12b. The main program and the heading for the procedure used.

```
Type the number for which you want the factorial
12
1!=1
2!=2
3!=6
4!=24
5!= 120
6!= 720
7!=5 040
8!=40 320
9!= 362 880
10!=3 628 800
11!=39 916 800
12!= 479 001 600
```

FIGURE 14.12c. Running the program of Figure 14.12b.